Rim Country Mountain Biking

RIM COUNTRY
MOUNTAIN
BIKING

Great Rides Along Arizona's Mogollon Rim

Jeffrey L. Stevenson

PRUETT PUBLISHING COMPANY
BOULDER, COLORADO

Printed in the United States
10 9 8 7 6 5 4 3 2 1

Library of Congress Cataloging-in-Publication data

Stevenson, Jeffrey L., 1959–
    Rim country mountain biking : great rides along Arizona's Mogollon
Rim / by Jeff Stevenson.
        p.   cm.
    Includes bibliographical references and index.
    ISBN 0-87108-856-8 (pbk.)
        1. All terrain cycling—Arizona—Tonto National Forest—
Guidebooks. 2. Tonto National Forest (Ariz.)—Guidebooks.
I. Title.
GV1045.5.A62T655   1995
796.6'4'09791—dc20   95-3546
                                                          CIP

Book design by Kathy McAffrey, Cover to Cover Design
Photographs by Jeffrey L. Stevenson and Beth Brannan Stevenson,
except photograph on page 17, courtesy of the Northern Gila County
Historical Society.
Cover photograph by Richard Wood/ProFiles West

To Dad for showing me
To Beth for supporting me
To Mom for encouraging me
To Brent and Dan for helping me
To Joe and Wes for going with me
To Davis and Matt, who I hope will learn to love it all.

Contents

Preface

I grew up with maps. My dad had been a member of the National Geographic Society since I had been born. Whenever he got a new map, we would spread it out on the floor and imagine traveling to every location on it that looked good. We watched every travel show we could find. After each show ended, we would get out the relevant maps and talk about how we might go there someday.

We used to travel together a lot. I would read highway maps and tell him about each town, river, and mountain we would pass along the way. Dad would take the car down old dirt roads in search of American Indian ruins, ranches, cemeteries, or new ways to get over a ridge without taking the highway. He worked for the airlines and we got to travel around the country visiting relatives. Dad was kind of a loner and would get bored with the family while on vacation, so he and I would take off in search of old cemeteries. We looked for the oldest headstones and would imagine what tragic tales could be told when family members died within a short time of each other. We would go to obscure little history museums and state parks. I always loved the sense of adventure trips like these offered.

When I became an adult Dad and I drifted apart. He died a tragic death when he was fifty-four, and it had been years since we shared an adventure together.

I used to go hiking a lot before I discovered mountain biking. I had a couple of good friends down in Tucson. I went backpacking with Joe Crews and biking with Wes Weisheit. We would buy topographic maps of some of the remote areas in southern Arizona and look for ranches, windmills, and ruins, and then we'd either hike or bike out to these places. We made some pretty amazing finds.

But then I got married and drifted away from my friends. I bought a mountain bike for my wife, Beth, and we moved to Payson, Arizona, where her mother lived. I bought some topographic maps of the area and looked for remote places to ride the bikes. We would load up the bikes with picnic lunches and bring along our dog. We would push and struggle along uninteresting roads that climbed hill after hill. Finally, we would decide to turn around after hawks started swooping our dog or some other disaster.

My work on this book began after one of these rides. I decided that I would never again take my wife on a ride without first showing her an elevation profile. I started making elevation profiles for each ride we planned so we would know what we were getting into. We looked up interesting places to visit and, after consulting the elevation profile, would cruise out to see them. We started compiling a load of information about the Rim Country, and I decided to share this information.

Many people travel through this area but never get off the beaten path. Yet the Mogollon Rim is one of the most interesting, diverse, and beautiful places in all of Arizona. This book is my attempt to share information about the Rim Country and to encourage you to explore it by mountain bike. Only by mountain bike can you smell the pine trees, hear the birds, feel the wind in your face, and experience the rush of a 30 MPH descent down a steep and rocky road.

Get on your bike and go! I will see you out there.

Acknowledgments

I would like to thank the following people for their help in preparing this book. Without their support, *Rim Country Mountain Biking* would be just another folder in my file cabinet.

Walt Thole, head of recreation for the Payson Ranger District, U.S. Forest Service, for helping me negotiate the government minefield, for providing extensive help preparing the maps, for answering my numerous questions, and for putting me in touch with others who have helped.

Wide World of Maps for their cartographic support.

George and Fern Spears of the Northern Gila County Historical Society for their help finding photos and providing valuable background information.

Diane Bain of the Arizona Mining and Mineral Museum for her patient help sorting through stacks of old mining reports to find interesting stories to tell.

Mary Rothschild, Frank Hoy, and Bill Jay of Arizona State University for their kind words and support while they were my instructors. Their encouragement helped me realize my writing potential.

My wife, Beth, for her unflinching critiques of my early work on this book (how many synonyms are there for climb and descend?).

Dan Basinski, local mountain bike hero, for his caustic encouragement, wayward directions, critical cultural analysis, and fine efforts at photo modeling.

John and Simone Lake of Manzanita Cycling for standing solidly behind cycling and my efforts, as well as providing photographs.

The Gila County Sheriff's Posse and the Tonto Rim Search and Rescue Squad for their medical and traffic control support at Payson cycling events.

Cliff Potts, Dave Lyons, Dale Menger, Becky Martinez, Al and Marci Valdini, Dave Price, Doris Frerichs, and all the other Payson merchants and business people for their continued support of Payson cycling.

Craig Swartwood and the Payson Chamber of Commerce for helping spread the good word about mountain biking to business people in the area.

Matt Hughey for being the only student of mine brave enough to go along on my explorations and for showing me how not to eat cactus fruit.

Finally, my two boys, Davis and Matthew, who, by their example, encourage me to want to learn as much about the world around me as I possibly can.

Introduction

Imagine 1,500 square miles of prime mountain biking territory: hundreds of miles of single-track trails, primitive jeep trails, remote logging roads, dirt roads, and well-groomed gravel roads, all within easy access of two state highways. This is the Mogollon Rim Country near and around Payson, Arizona. The area this book covers extends from the towns of Rye to Forest Lakes, Arizona. It is centered in Payson and the Rim Lakes Recreation Area, around Woods Canyon Lake. Elevations range from 2,500 to 8,000 feet. The region is home to stands of aspen, spruce, and fir trees, vast ponderosa pine forests, oak and juniper woodlands, and it includes sections of the Sonora Desert, with its stately saguaro cactus. The animal life reflects the wide variety of habitats.

You can still see evidence of four prehistoric American Indian cultures that once lived in the Payson area, and you can ride to some of their former battle sites. You will also come across ruins of towns, forts, mining camps, and many old ranches.

The area's geologic history is diverse, too. It offers everything from Precambrian mountain ranges to Tertiary lava flows. You can hunt for fossils or scramble across huge piles of granite boulders. You can bike to swimming holes, gushing springs, deep canyons, high plateaus, rugged mountains, and fantastic views.

This is mountain bike heaven.

The area covered in this book is in two of the most visited national forests in the country, the Tonto and the Apache-Sitgreaves National Forests. Fortunately, most forest visitors do not venture beyond a couple of tourist spots. If you take your mountain bike just past these places, you will find yourself in beautiful and remote country.

Although this book is primarily a mountain biking guide, it includes information for the casual forest visitor. Throughout the book you will find information on the region's flora, fauna, geology, and human history.

The first part of *Rim Country Mountain Biking* provides a brief overview of the ecologic zones, geologic periods, and human history of the area. There is also a section on biking safety and the weather. The main part of the book is devoted to the bike route descriptions. These are grouped by location. To get a complete picture of a ride, read the section introduction and the route descriptions of other rides in the vicinity.

Each description features a list that profiles the route:

Highlights: Describes the best things about the route.

Seasons: Suggests the best time of year to explore the route. Many of the rides in this book can be done year-round.

Distance: Provides approximate round-trip distance for the route, whether around a loop, or out and back.

Time: Estimates the time it will take a relatively fit rider to complete the route. Depending upon your level of fitness, biking ability, the weather, and if you like to explore, rides may be longer or shorter than times listed.

Difficulty Rating: Each ride is rated as *very easy, easy, moderate, difficult,* or *strenuous.* The routes designated *very easy* are short, easy to follow, well-maintained, and suitable for the novice mountain biker. *Easy* rides are somewhat longer, rougher, and may be more difficult to follow, but they are still suitable for beginners.

A *moderate* rating designates longer easy rides, easy rides with technical sections, or shorter technical rides. These rides are suitable for beginners who have some mountain biking experience as well as for advanced riders.

Difficult rides are longer and may have some technical sections, steep hills, sections that require some route finding skill, and are generally for experienced mountain bikers.

Strenuous rides are all-day workouts. They are steep, remote, and include lengthy sections of technical riding (or pushing). They should only be attempted by fit mountain bikers who have backcountry experience.

High and **Low Elevation:** Specifies the highest and lowest points on the ride.

United States Geological Survey (USGS) Topographic Maps: Names the USGS 1:24,000 (7-1/2 minute series) maps that correspond to the routes. While there are maps in the book, additional topographic maps are recommended—you will need them both. Topo maps are available from sporting goods and map stores, including

Wide World of Maps in Phoenix. Note that the USGS maps cannot keep up with the number of roads and trails that have been created over the years, so even the most recent issues may not show all of the trails listed in this book. Still, there is no substitute for these maps to help you gain a good idea of the lay of the land.

Connecting Rides: Identifies other rides that intersect with this ride, if there are any. Use this information to customize rides or to learn more about the ride you are on. Be careful when you add to your ride that you do not stray too far away from your final destination, or extend it beyond your physical limitations.

Access: Provides general directions to the start of the ride from the intersection of Arizona Highways 87 and 260 in the middle of Payson. All rides start and end at the access point.

Elevation Profile: This chart illustrates how steep the hills are along the route. Chart elevations are drawn on the same scale, meaning the elevation profiles of easy rides show a fairly flat line while the profiles of strenuous rides might look like an old broken comb. The higher the hills, the taller the elevation profile. Distance along the bottom of the profile varies depending on the length of the ride.

Route Description: This describes the route terrain. It includes cumulative mileage distances, forest service road numbers, and important landmarks along the route. This information is as accurate as possible, but please remember that landmarks change, familiar routes can wash out, and new roads can be cut. Use your common sense— and good maps—when following the routes.

Notes: Offers some brief information about the geology, history, and ecology of the route. Readers interested in learning more about the Rim Country and the outdoors can refer to the bibliography.

Finally, be sure to check out the appendices. While I have tried to make this guide as complete as possible, sometimes you will want more information. The people and organizations listed in Appendix A (For Further Information) will be happy to help you with any questions you might have. Appendix B (Rides Grouped by Difficulty) will help you select rides appropriate to your fitness level.

Safety in the Rim Country: What to Know Before You Go

The weather in the Rim Country can be extreme. It can be as hot as 115° F—in the shade—at lower elevations in summer, or as cold as −10° F at higher elevations in winter. Because the Rim Country is an arid region, it is not uncommon for temperatures to vary as much as 40° F from day to night. A beautiful afternoon can quickly become a freezing night. Many people have died from hypothermia in the Rim Country.

Always be prepared for the worst. Bring extra clothing so if you do break down or get lost and can't get back to shelter you won't freeze. A jacket, extra shirt, and sweat pants will help you survive a night outdoors. If you have to spend the night out, be sure to take off your sweaty clothes and put on dry ones. Stay out of the wind. Find shelter behind rocks or vegetation. Bring matches. Even the coldest nights are tolerable if you build a fire.

Water can be a problem. Even when it is cool you will use a lot of water so be sure to carry plenty with you. Never drink the water you find in the wild without purifying it first as it is nearly always contaminated. I carry purification tablets or a water filter/pump in case of emergencies.

I have extra water bottle cages all over my bike. I carry a gallon of water whenever I ride. Some people carry extra water in "piggyback" water systems. A partially filled collapsible water jug strapped to your rack is another way to carry extra water. I drink that water first, then stuff the jug into my pannier.

The weather is usually nice year-round. Late summer, from mid-July through September, is monsoon season in the Rim Country. The monsoons are created by a weather pattern that brings warm moist air up from the Pacific Ocean and the Gulf of California. As warm air is pushed up over the Rim, giant thunderclouds begin to build by mid-day. These clouds can unleash thunderstorms of tremendous fury.

Temperatures can drop 30° F within minutes, wind can gust to 60 MPH, rain can be ice cold, and hail can be the size of golf balls. Lightning strikes are numerous. The storms usually move off the edge of the Rim and head south. If you are riding during the monsoons, be sure to carry something that can keep you dry. I carry a plastic emergency poncho that weighs about an ounce.

If lightning is striking nearby, do not take shelter under a large tree, as they attract lightning. Stay away from rock outcroppings, hillsides, streams, and washes. The safest place to be when lightning is striking is in a grove of trees or a dense forest. Get away from your metal bike. If you are not near a thick grove of trees, crouch down in a low-lying area with your feet close together touching the ground.

Thunderstorms also bring flash floods, common in the Rim Country. When it pours rain over a short time, the ground can't soak up the water. The water gushes into the nearest wash and soon it can be roaring. I have seen a flash flood. There were thunderstorms all around and it had rained about a half hour before. The sun was out and the creek was just a trickle. Then I saw it. The flood looked like a breaker at the seashore after the curl has crashed. It was a foaming brown mess about two feet high, full of debris. This was a small flood, but it would have been dangerous had I been in the creek bottom, or had I not seen it coming.

If thunderstorms are in the area, particularly if they are upstream from you, stay out of the creeks and washes. Even if it is not raining where you are, a flash flood can occur. *Never cross a flooded creek.* If you are riding during thunderstorm season, cross creeks and washes rapidly. If you are cut off by a flood, just relax. The water usually recedes as fast as it comes up.

Nonmonsoon storms present other problems. They can move in and stay for a couple of days, dropping a lot of rain or snow. When streams rise from these storms, they can stay high for a few days, especially in the springtime when a warm rain can melt the snowpack quickly. Fortunately, these storms happen infrequently.

Be prepared for emergencies. Carry a first aid kit and know how to use it. If you are not knowledgeable about first aid, carry a first aid book with you. You should also carry a whistle and a signal mirror.

Make sure that your bike is in good working order. Carry basic tools you may need to fix your bike and be prepared for flat tires. You may want to carry an extra folding tire along with your spare tubes. I carry a pair of pliers, an adjustable wrench, allen wrenches to fit all the bolts on the bike, a chain repair tool, a bottom bracket tool, a screwdriver, a patch kit, two spare tubes, extra bolts, and duct tape (you'd be surprised how far you can ride on a shredded tire reinforced with duct tape). Always try to ride with at least two other people. That way, if someone gets hurt, one person can go for help and the other can stay with the injured person. Always let someone know where you are going and when you plan to be back. If you don't return on time, they can notify authorities.

Tread lightly with your bike by staying on the roads and trails. There are plenty of them; you don't have to make new ones. Don't cut switchbacks. Yield to hikers and horses. Don't speed into a blind corner where you might run into someone not expecting you. Don't litter. In fact, pack out more litter than you came in with.

Safety concerns are paramount in the Rim Country. In 1972 thirteen people were killed when a flash flood roared down Tonto Creek without warning. In 1990 six firefighters were killed battling the Dude Creek fire. In 1994 a man was killed by lightning on Willow Springs Lake.

Even experienced riders who are familiar with the terrain of the Rim Country can get lost, and those who venture out ill-prepared for whatever weather they might encounter can suffer potentially serious, even fatal consequences.

The rides covered in this book are in rugged and remote country; they are not "rides in the park." Make sure that you are prepared before you head out.

What Is the Rim Country? A Brief Look at Its Geology, Ecology, and History

Geology

The history of the Rim Country begins about two billion years ago, when the area was at the southwest of a large continent. Layers of volcanic rock from ash and lava flows, interspersed with sedimentary rock from rivers, lakes, and oceans, were deposited at this time.

About 1.8 billion years ago a huge pool of molten lava formed under the area and pushed up the older, harder rocks, forming mountains that were then taller than the present-day Himalayas. This mountain building lasted about 200 million years and is known as the Mazatzal Revolution. The pool of lava at the core of the mountains eventually cooled, hardened, and became granite. Most of the granite exposed in the Rim Country was formed at this time.

Between 1.6 and 1.2 billion years ago these giant mountains eroded to a flat plain, as did much of the earth, and from 1.2 billion to 600 million years ago the Rim Country was lifted up and worn down once again. From 600 to 240 million years ago the ocean inundated the western half of what is now Arizona several times. Each time the ocean advanced, more sedimentary rock was deposited. When the ocean retreated, the land was raised up very little and minimal erosion occurred.

Between 225 and 100 million years ago, what is now southern Arizona was raised to form a large mountain range. Sediment from these mountains washed down and forged a wide plain at the edge of the ocean, which covered the Rim Country at the time.

From 80 to 40 million years ago there was extensive faulting throughout Arizona. Some areas were pushed up while other areas dropped down, forming basins. Some of these basins, such as the Tonto Basin south of Payson, held water that had no outlet to the oceans and large, salty lakes formed. Sediment from the surrounding mountains washed into the basins and slowly filled them in. It was during this time that the first pine forests grew.

Between 30 and 20 million years ago there was yet another period of mountain building. The Colorado Plateau rose up, with the Mogollon Rim at its edge (the plateau stretches north to the Four Corners area, west to the Verde River valley, and east to New Mexico). Surprisingly, this area did not change significantly for millions of years. During all subsequent periods of mountain building in Arizona, the Colorado Plateau "floated" on top of the earth's mantle like a raft.

There was also extensive volcanic activity throughout Arizona 30 to 20 million years ago. The most important event to occur near the Rim Country was the explosion of the Superstition Mountains near Phoenix. Even closer, the small volcano now called Baker Butte erupted near the edge of the Rim northeast of the present-day town of Pine.

Over the past 20 million years the Rim has continued to erode, the edge moving about 10 miles north of its original location, and the Tonto Basin filling with sediment. The Salt River eventually broke through its landlocked basin via its present-day channel in what must have been a tremendous flood.

What does all this have to do with mountain biking? Basically there are three types of rock, each offering different riding characteristics: *extrusive igneous, intrusive igneous,* and *sedimentary.* Extrusive igneous rock is formed by lava flows or ash falls on the earth's surface. In the Rim Country, rocks from lava flows are hard, dark, and jagged, offering a harsh, unforgiving terrain for mountain bikers. Rocks formed from ash look much like sedimentary rocks.

Intrusive igneous rock is formed when huge chambers of molten rock cool underground and harden, becoming granite. Granite is exposed when surface rock layers wear away. The sun heats and expands the surface of the rock while the core remains cool, causing the outer layer to peel off, much like an onion skin. Boulder piles are formed when water and exfoliation expand the natural cracks within a granite mass. At the base of the boulders the granite breaks into blocks that eventually weather into coarse sand, which can be very slippery to ride on.

Rim Country Mountain Biking

"Egg Rock" is typical of the large granite boulders found in the Rim Country.

Sedimentary rock is formed when bits and pieces, or sediment, of older rock are washed down and deposited by water. The sediment is spread in broad horizontal sheets and eventually becomes rock when the water is squeezed out and the debris bonds together under the enormous pressure of the continually accumulating sediment above.

The way sedimentary rock weathers will affect your riding in different ways. The harder sedimentary rock, for example, may break into pieces ranging in size from ping-pong balls to basketballs, forcing you to push through some areas. Limestone is weathered when rainwater, made slightly acidic from the carbon dioxide it collects as it falls through the atmosphere, chemically dissolves part of the rock. Tiny gullies, called *grikes,* form where the water has dissolved the rock, and three-to-four-inch pinnacles, called *clints,* form between the grikes. You will know you are riding on limestone when you and your bike take a beating as you cross over stretches of light-colored clints.

The Rim Country is a geologic wonderland and you can find evidence of it on every ride you take.

Ecology

The Rim Country contains a complex web of life zones. Each zone contains common plant and animal species that are found in relatively even distribution. These plants and animals are different in each zone. Life zones span higher on north-facing slopes and lower in cool shaded valleys. Zones are lower on south-facing slopes and ridges that get a lot of sun. Because of the complex system of ridges and canyons in this area you will pass in and out of several different life zones as you ride.

Boundries between zones are called *ecotones.* An ecotone contains plant and animal species from each of the zones along its boundary. This makes ecotones ideal places to view wildlife. Because the life zones here are so intermingled, almost the entire Rim Country can be considered an ecotone between two or more life zones.

There are eight life zones, or habitats, in the Rim Country: the Upland Sonora Desert, grasslands, brushlands, riparian, piñon and juniper woodlands, ponderosa pine forests, mixed conifer forests, and aspen stands.

Upland Sonora Desert
This is the "youngest" habitat. The desert as we know it probably migrated north from Mexico about ten thousand years ago. The Sonoran Desert is the most diverse desert in North America, growing in three "layers." The first layer consists of plants and cactus that are less than eighteen inches tall, the second layer of medium-sized brush and cactus that grow between eighteen and thirty-six inches, and the third layer of trees and saguaros that reach three feet or more in height.

There is only one ride in this guidebook that will take you into this habitat. Common plants include mesquite and palo verde trees as well as the trademark saguaros. The beaver tail, or "prickly pear," and the century plant can be located at higher elevations.

Grasslands

Grasslands in the Rim Country occur at higher elevations than the Upland Sonoran Desert. This habitat is marked by the predominance of blue/grey grama grasses, bunch grass, and the ever-present fox tails as well as the scarcity of bushes, although you will find clumps of brush or cactus throughout the grasslands.

Brushlands

Brushlands occur where it is too dry for piñon or juniper trees to grow or where it is too rocky for grasslands to take hold. The main brush in this habitat is chaparral. It consists of several low-lying, compact, and drought-resistant species such as manzanita and scrub oak. Brushlands are widespread at lower elevations of the Rim Country.

Piñon and Juniper Woodlands

Where it is a little moister the brushlands and grasslands give way to piñon and juniper trees. The trees are generally shorter than thirty feet and tend to clump together, though their crowns do not touch. The trees are slow-growing and resistant to drought and cold. In fact, piñons are one of the slowest growing pine trees. Woodlands are widespread in the Rim Country and seem to be favored by humans, perhaps because they provide shady spaces and sunny spots.

Riparian

This habitat occurs where there is permanent moisture, as along rivers, streams, or washbeds. Undergrowth is often thick and lush. Here you'll find large sycamore and cottonwood trees that require hundreds of gallons of water a day to grow. Riparian areas offer a remarkable splash of vivid green at the lower elevations, where plant life otherwise tends to be shades of brown and green.

Ponderosa Pine Forest

This is the Rim Country's most extensive habitat. In fact, the Rim Country anchors the southern edge of the largest ponderosa pine forest in the world. Ponderosa pine forests grow in the warmest and driest

A giant ponderosa pine reaches for the Arizona sky.

spots that conifer (or pine) forests can grow, and intermingle with brushlands and woodland species at lower elevations and other conifers at higher elevations. Understory is not very thick because the trees use up so much of the nutrients in the soil. At lower elevations, trees will be widely spaced apart. When trees get older, the bark changes in color from a rugged black to a smooth yellow.

The ponderosa pine is the most common pine tree in North America. It is the most valuable commercial tree in the western United

States, as the wood is good for building window and door frames. The ponderosa is also known as "yellow pine" because of the way the bark thickens and becomes yellow as it grows older. Huge yellow pines are hard to come by, as they are the most valuable to loggers. Logging, however, has been slowed due to new environmental laws and the closing of the sawmill in Payson in the summer of 1993. The ponderosa pine was named in 1826 by David Douglas, a Scottish botanical explorer, who thought the wood was very heavy, or "ponderous."

Mixed Conifer Forests

At higher elevations, stands of pure ponderosa pines intermix with Douglas fir and various types of spruce trees. Spruce and fir trees are not as hardy as the ponderosa pine, so their range is limited to areas that are prime conifer habitats.

Aspen Forest

Aspen forests grow in areas that have been burned or logged. They are known as "pioneer trees" because they give way to other species more suited to the area. The trees also grow in narrow bands around meadows. Aspen trees grow very fast, reaching heights of ten feet in only six to eight years. Although aspen trees produce seeds, they are unlikely to reproduce this way. Rather, their roots extend out near the surface and smaller trees, called "suckers," grow up from the roots. Eventually the suckers form their own root system. Aspen stands clone from one or more trees, making them susceptible to disease and parasites.

Fires

Fires are an important part of the Rim Country ecosystem. Before Europeans came, American Indians would periodically set fires to clear out the underbrush in the forests. These fires would prevent the brushlands from becoming too thick and helped improve the forage for larger animals such as deer and elk. Fires sparked by lightning also helped clear out underbrush. Most of these fires were cool and close to the ground. Very rarely would they reach the crowns of the trees and destroy them. Large trees were left standing, and they flourished.

When settlers moved into the western United States in the late nineteenth century, they were careless and there were a number of huge and disastrous fires. The newly created U.S. Forest Service, in response to the public outcry over these large fires, instituted a policy of strict fire suppression. Unfortunately, not only were the destructive crown fires suppressed, but the beneficial ground fires as well. This allowed the understory and brush to grow very thick, and fires that were once cool and constructive became immediately hot, destructive, and often times uncontrollable. In the 1970s, the Forest Service began to see the error of its ways and changed its policies. Controlled burns were set to help clear out some of the thick underbrush. Still, most of the Rim Country is thicker with trees now than it was 150 years ago.

Logging practices in the area have also caused fire problems. When Europeans first came into the area they noticed how huge and widely spaced the trees were in the forests and compared the forests to parks. They began cutting down the trees to build things. Thick stands of trees grew in the areas that had been cleared, resulting in areas with trees that are about the same age and grow very close together. This creates an environment where destructive crown fires can start easily because the crowns of the trees touch.

Forest fires do not burn uniformly. Some areas within the burned perimeter burn to the ground, scorching the topsoil, while other areas remain completely untouched by the fire. Between these extremes are every degree of burn, helping to create a variety of habitats within the burned area. This diversity helps the forest recover and even flourish after a fire.

In the brushlands, chaparral *needs* fire to grow. Without fire, the brush becomes burdened by dead material. In fact, there may be more dead material than living. Fires burn away dead growth so that the plant can thrive.

You will see many examples of uncontrolled fire damage in the Rim Country as well as many areas thick with underbrush or closely packed trees that are overdue for a fire.

Human History

In the generally accepted theory of human history, there were periods of time when a land bridge connected Asia and North America. Humans migrated from Asia to North America in search of big game to hunt. They slowly moved into North and South America and populated the continents.

The earliest humans in the Rim Country we now refer to as Paleo-Indians, and they may have been here as early as thirty-eight thousand years ago. The region was warmer and wetter than it is now and these people lived by hunting the big game that roamed here. About seven thousand years ago the climate began to dry and the big game disappeared. The Paleo-Indians were forced to give up big game hunting and turn to gathering wild plants to supplement their food supplies.

Between seven thousand and two thousand years ago, the Rim Country was inhabited by the Desert, or Cochise, People who mainly subsisted on hunting and gathering. They were introduced to corn from Mexico about forty-five hundred years ago, which helped them supplement their diet with a more dependable source of food. These people developed the *mano-y-metate*, a stone tool used for grinding corn and other grains, as well as pottery for storing food. They established permanent settlements centered around farming.

Between 300 B.C. and 500 A.D. people migrated north from Mexico, where there was a well-developed culture, and brought new ideas to the Rim Country. The first culture to evolve from this migration was the Mogollon. The people of this culture lived east of the Rim Country toward the White Mountains. They subsisted by hunting and gathering in the rich environment where they lived. To the northeast, the Anasazi culture developed. These people built cliff dwellings and used dry farming techniques.

The Hohokam culture developed in the deserts southwest of the Rim Country. These people learned to use irrigation and established large communities in the lower desert valleys. The Hohokam built two- and three-room dwellings in the Rim Country. The Sinagua culture developed around present-day Flagstaff, and these people migrated south to the Verde Valley after the eruption of Sunset Crater in 1065.

With few "permanent" inhabitants, the Rim Country was more like a highway than anything else. It was a popular trade route for each of these cultures.

About 1000 A.D., there was a cultural shift in the Rim Country when the people living here began to build pueblo-style villages. Many of the American Indian village ruins you see around the Rim Country were built during this time. Different pottery techniques were introduced from around the region and there is evidence of extensive trade. The civilization here reached its peak in about 1150 A.D.

By the end of the thirteenth century, the civilization appears to have declined and the Rim Country was nearly abandoned. Archaeologists are unsure why this happened but speculate that an extended drought (lasting from 1276 to 1299) may have contributed to the human exodus. There is also evidence of shifts to building more defensible villages in the region, which suggests there may have been extensive warfare as people competed for diminishing food and water sources. Whatever the reason, the Rim Country appeared to be empty of people until the 1500s.

During the 1400s a new influx of people—Athabaskins—migrated into the Arizona region from Canada. These people probably moved south along the Front Range of the Rockies and then into northern New Mexico and Arizona through the passes around present-day Gallup, New Mexico. Two American Indian tribes evolved from this new wave of migration: the Navajo of the Four Corners region and the Apache of central and eastern Arizona. There is evidence that the first Apache tribes came to the Rim Country during the late 1500s.

The northern Apache became dependent on raiding as a way of life. They lived in the mountains and attacked other tribes who lived in more settled communities of the Rio Grande Valley and south-central Arizona. The Apache of the Rim Country, however, were farther from these settlements, so they turned to farming and were much less nomadic than their cousins. They became known as the "Tonto" Apaches.

Although the Spanish and, later, the Mexicans arrived in Arizona between the sixteenth and nineteenth centuries, there is little evidence that they came into the Rim Country. This area was, and is, remote and rugged. The presence of the Apache in the mountains around the Rim Country also made it a dangerous place to travel.

The first documented European to enter the area was Antoine Leroux, a guide for the Lt. Amiel Weeks Whiple expedition, who traveled up the East Verde River in 1854. There may have been some brief explorations in years prior by trappers in search of beaver, but there is no documented evidence of this.

During the Civil War, much of the military was sent east to fight in that great conflict. The Apache took the opportunity to step up their attacks on the American settlements.

After the war the military returned to Arizona determined to end all conflict with the Apache. One of the main difficulties of the Rim Country was traveling across it without being attacked. In 1871, Gen. O. O. Howard was sent by the War Department to make peace with

Early miners, friends, and family pose outside a mining shack.

them. He assigned Gen. George Crook to keep the Apache confined to reservations. General Crook also oversaw the construction of the General Crook Trail, which extended from Fort Whipple (near present-day Prescott) to Fort Apache, on what is now the White Mountain Apache Reservation. This trail followed the edge of the Rim and was the first road through the area.

The Apache were subdued and the Rim Country was thrown open to settlers. Some of the very first settlers were Mormons, seeking to expand their Salt Lake City empire by establishing farming communities in Arizona. Heber and Pine were settled as part of this Mormon expansion.

There were mining strikes around Payson during the 1870s, and during the 1870s and 1880s hundreds of mining claims were taken out in the Rim Country. Almost none of the mines made a substantial profit, but they served to help bring settlers to the area.

Concurrent with the mining boom was the introduction of cattle into the Rim Country. The area was filled with tall grass and lush vegetation ideal for raising cattle. By the 1880s, the area was packed with cattle, perhaps by as much as twenty times the number of cattle allowed to graze here now.

Sheep were also brought in and some of the sheep ranches rivaled the cattle ranches in size and revenues. For the most part, the sheep were kept on top of the Rim. Violence erupted in the 1880s when some sheep ranchers tried to bring sheep down from the Rim. Cattle ranchers opposed this because sheep crop grasses too close to the ground, making it difficult for cattle to graze. It took until 1892 for all of the sheep to be driven back to the top of the Rim, but not before 29 people had been killed in what became known as the Pleasant Valley War.

Overgrazing, falling beef prices, and an extended drought caused the collapse of the Rim Country's cattle industry about 1905. The land eroded rapidly and population growth slowed considerably, though people continued to ranch into the twentieth century. During Prohibition, ranchers profited by distilling bootleg liquor. It has been noted that Payson moonshine was well-known from as far away as Los Angeles.

The Beeline Highway was built in 1937 and connected the Rim Country with the rest of the state. Before the construction of the highway, freight hauling was a difficult, but profitable, business as nearly everything not made on area ranches had to be brought in from somewhere else.

The lumber industry also started soon after the settlers arrived. Several small sawmills were set up and practically everything they manufactured was made of pine boards. The industry was stimulated during World War II and more people were drawn to the area.

During the 1950s Woods Canyon Lake was constructed and people began to come to the Rim Country for recreation. Inexpensive land and a mild climate attracted retirees. There are a substantial number of retirees living here now.

As the population of Phoenix and the Valley of the Sun increased, more people poured into the Rim Country. During the 1970s and 1980s the Beeline Highway was improved and camping facilities were expanded. A major campground just north of Payson is scheduled to open in the spring of 1996.

Although residents of the Rim Country hope to expand the economic base of the area through clean industry, such as small medical and electronics manufacturing plants, it would seem that the future of this area rests with tourism.

PAYSON

The area around town is marked by short, steep hills that create numerous microecologic zones. Look for ponderosa pine forests on the north sides of hills and in the cooler low-lying valleys. The south and west slopes are covered with brush and grasslands that include patches of piñon and juniper woodlands. Despite the fact that Payson is rapidly becoming a small urban area, there is a wide diversity of wildlife.

Geologically, the area is almost completely granite. There are huge granite monoliths, giant boulder piles, troughs of broken rocky debris, and layers of deep, coarse sand.

Payson became the center of population in the Rim Country because of its close proximity to mines, forests (for lumber), and grazing land. Payson continues to grow, and evidence of urban sprawl can be seen on nearly every ride. Don't be discouraged though. Just a few minutes on any of these trails and you will be in areas as remote as you want them to be.

 **1. Stewart Pocket**

Highlights: Granite Dells, "roller coaster road"

Seasons: All year, hot in summer

Distance: 7.3 miles

Time: 2 hours

Difficulty Rating: Moderate

High Elevation: 5,000 feet   **Low Elevation:** 4,560 feet

USGS Topographic Maps: Payson South

Access: Turn east on Arizona 260. Park in the Walmart parking lot just past the intersection.

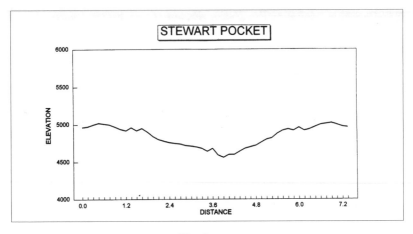

The Route

Cross Highway 260 at the stoplight at the southeast corner of the parking lot. This is Granite Dells Road. Follow the paved road as it turns to the east, over a couple of rises and into the forest.

At the bottom of the first good hill you will pass by a gate to your right. Just down this private road is a very old, spring-fed apple

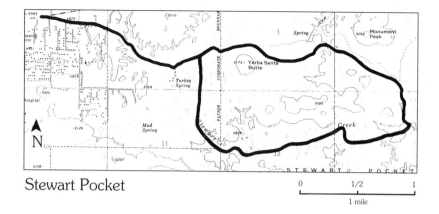

Stewart Pocket

0   1/2   1

1 mile

orchard. Climb up the small hill to the intersection of Sutton Road (1.3 miles) and turn right onto the dirt road.

Sutton Road is known as "roller coaster road," and you are on top of the first big hill. There are four hills in the next quarter mile, each a little lower than the one before. If you can control your bike and are brave enough, you can catch some air going *over* the tops of these hills. Just watch for cars coming the other way.

At the bottom of the last hill the road makes a sharp turn to the right. Fortunately it is signed, so you can slow down in time to make the corner. Just past this turn, take the first trail on your left (1.9 miles). You will be in a sandy wash, but after about 50 yards come to a well-defined jeep trail. Follow this trail to your left, downstream.

Continue on this sandy trail into a ponderosa pine forest inter-mixed with a lot of oak trees. Pass through the fence line. The area to your left was burned out a few years ago in a small forest fire.

Drop into the creek bottom and follow it downstream. You will come to a fork in the trail where the creek has washed it out. Vehicles have cut a trail to your right that goes up and over the little hill, but you can go straight ahead. Either way will get you back on course after a couple of yards.

As you descend down the canyon you will cross the creek several times and the ponderosas will begin to thin out. Soon you will come to a spot where the trail seems to disappear and the stream is pinched off by some large boulders (3.4 miles). Walk your bike into the creek bottom and look for the trail that climbs out the other side, directly opposite of you. Do not try to follow the creek down as it leads to a series of drop-offs.

Climb up the steep trail through the manzanita to the top of the hill. (This is probably a push.) The trail comes up between two big piles of boulders. Cross over the top of the hill. Head toward the east where you see a ranch and some powerlines. The descent is steep, narrow, and slippery, and you go in and out of a wash a couple of times. Be sure to follow the trail; do not turn off into the wash. If you find yourself starting to slide down the hill, get off and walk the bike to help keep the trail from becoming too rutted.

At the next hill, climb toward the big pile of boulders to your right. Just beneath the rocks, the trail traverses to the east. Follow this trail high above the creek bottom, up and over the saddle to your right. Drop down into the steep, sandy wash (3.9 miles). Climb out of the wash straight across to the other side, into Stewart Pocket.

Turn to your right to get into the Granite Dells and check out the boulder piles. Head up the main road to your left to leave Stewart Pocket. Follow this road uphill for about 2 miles until you get to the top. The big hill to your left, close to the road, is Yerba Sentra Butte. Just past this spot the road descends gently and you can scream back to the paved road and head back to Walmart.

Notes

The stream crossing at Granite Dells is an excellent place to study some geology. You can see where the water has dug this wash deeper and deeper, cutting away the stream bank to the north. You may even be able to see where the creek has eroded the root structure of a tree, allowing it to topple into the wash. This wash drains the southeast Payson geographic area. Runoff increases as more houses are built because the houses take up ground that would normally allow the water to soak in. As Payson grows, more and more water will pour through here, making the wash deeper and wider.

The ranch located in Granite Dells is a private ranch. Currently, it serves as a drug rehabilitation center, but it was originally established in 1888 by Ben and Sarah Stewart. This valley is named Stewart Pocket after them.

The Stewarts were married in Mason County, Texas, in 1861, before Ben went off to join the Confederates in the Civil War. He was captured and imprisoned in the North where he developed chronic bronchitis. After the war he moved back to Mason County, but then

An example of severe erosion at a stream crossing in Granite Dells.

came to Arizona to help improve his health. The Stewarts traveled from Texas by wagon train with the Young family, who homesteaded about 30 miles east of Payson in the Pleasant Valley. The Youngs raised alfalfa, fruit, and vegetables on the ranch to use at a hotel and livery stable they bought in Payson. They sold the ranch in 1909 and spent the rest of their years visiting relatives.

# 2. Peach Orchard Springs

Highlights: Mine ruins, Peach Orchard Springs

Seasons: All year, hot in summer

Distance: 5.4 miles

Time: 2 hours

Difficulty Rating: Moderate

High Elevation: 5,100 feet **Low Elevation:** 4,640 feet

USGS Topographic Maps: Payson South

Connecting Rides: 3. Snowstorm Mountain, 6. Cypress Thicket, 7. Doll Baby Ranch, 8. Marysville Hill

Access: Head south on Arizona 87 about 1 mile until it intersects with Main Street. Turn west on Main Street and follow it through downtown about 1 mile to the Museum of the Forest.

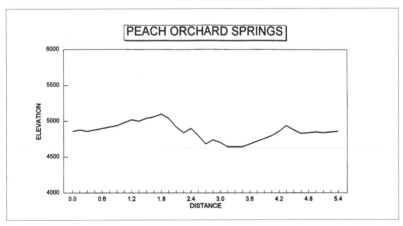

The Route

Begin by riding back east on Main Street. When you get to the heart of Main Street turn right on McLane Road (0.3 mile). Follow McLane south out of town.

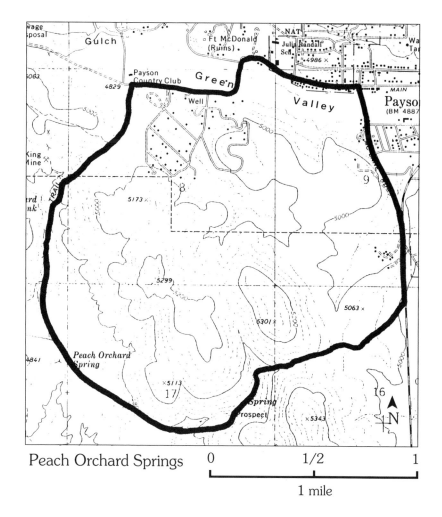

Peach Orchard Springs

0   1/2   1

1 mile

When you get to Highway 87 (1.0 mile), follow it to the south (the shoulder is wide, so you won't have to compete for space with cars). Follow Highway 87 past the Mazatzal Casino and down a short hill. Look for the power lines on the opposite side of the highway. About 100 yards past the "Town of Payson" (TOP) marker are the gate and road you are looking for. Turn west here (1.3 miles).

Go through the gate and follow the well-defined jeep trail. The trail is immediately rocky and climbs steadily toward the saddle straight ahead (1.8 miles).

The descent is very steep and rocky. Once you pass through the fence line the trail narrows. There are a couple of switchbacks before you drop to the creek bottom, where you will find ruins of a mining cabin (2.4 miles). Continue through the gate down the creek and in about 100 yards you come to old abandoned mining prospects. No tunnels were made here. Rather, the ground was "scooped out" to get to the minerals.

Just past the mine, cross the stream and climb up a steep hill to the ridge line. As you climb, notice the mine tailings to the left. When you reach the top of this hill you will be able to see cone-shaped Mount Ord, with its towers, off to your left (2.7 miles).

After descending the steep rocky hill you will come to a well-maintained Forest Service road. Turn right here, cross the creek bottom, and climb up the hill. Contour to the north around the hill a bit and then begin a fast descent into Peach Orchard Springs, with its many tall trees.

The riparian vegetation around the springs is lush and is a nice place to stop if the weather is hot (3.2 miles). The main road goes right through the trees, but at the far side of the grove make a right turn into the creek bottom, away from the main road that climbs up and off to your left.

Follow the creek bottom for about 50 yards. The trail climbs out of the creek on your right and passes through an area thick with brush. In a quarter of a mile you will come out onto FS 441, a dirt road. Turn right.

Follow this road up and over the saddle (4.3 miles). When you reach the top of the hill, you will see the houses of Payson all around. Descend this hill, head through the gate, and return to paved road at the Payson Golf Course (4.6 miles). Turn right and follow this paved road back to the museum.

Notes

The Payson area was settled in 1882 under the name Union Park. John and Frank Hise opened a general store near present-day downtown to serve the mining districts to the west. Their father came to visit from Chicago and was appalled at the poor postal service. He wrote Congressman Louis Edward Payson, then chairman of the House Committee on Post Offices, and requested a post office for the

Exploring mine ruins on the way to Peach Orchard Springs.

town. A post office was established in March 1884, and it was run by Frank Hise. They named the post office Payson in honor of the congressman.

During the 1920s Guy and Irene Barkdoll owned a ranch and a peach orchard at the springs. Their son Lee attended school in Payson, but he apparently did not like it because he kept trying to escape out the window. The teacher warned him three times to stop climbing out the window before she strapped him. Irene was so upset that she petitioned to have the teacher fired. Though the school board voted "no" on the firing, the teacher died of a heart attack before she heard the verdict.

Just across the street from the historical museum is Julia Randall Elementary School. It was built in the early part of the twentieth century and named after a first grade teacher who taught in Payson forty-six years before retiring in 1969.

3. Snowstorm Mountain

Highlights: Excellent views to the west, American Gulch
Seasons: All year, hot in summer
Distance: 10.9 miles
Time: 4 hours
Difficulty Rating: Difficult
High Elevation: 5,290 feet **Low Elevation:** 3,960 feet
USGS Topographic Maps: Payson South, North Peak, Buckhead Mesa,
Payson North
Connecting Rides: 2. Peach Orchard Springs, 6. Cypress Thicket, 7. Doll
Baby Ranch, 8. Marysville Hill
Access: Head south on Highway 87 about 1 mile to the intersection of
Arizona 87 and Main Street. Turn west on Main Street and go
through downtown until you come to the Payson Country Club golf
course, about 1.5 miles. Park at the golf club.

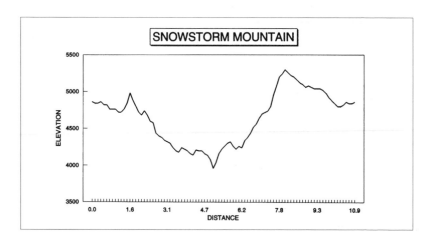

Snowstorm Mountain

0   1/2   1

1 mile

The Route

Go past the country club and onto the dirt road. After 200 yards you will pass the entrance to the sewage treatment plant, and then meet up with and follow the American Gulch, crossing it twice.

The route climbs up the hill to the left while the American Gulch swings off to the north. Climb this steep hill. Snowstorm Mountain is the rounded, brush-covered hill to your right as you climb. Descend the steep rocky section of the hill, then cross a low, rutted, sometimes muddy area. Follow the main road up a short hill to the saddle. Marysville Hill will be to your left. The road will drop away quickly from this point and is steep and rocky.

In the middle of your screaming descent you pass a road to your left marked "Cypress Thicket" (3 miles). Keep to the right here and look for FS 67, in about 1 mile. Turn right on FS 67 (3.9 miles) and head north. There are a couple of steep, rocky, but short hills here. Cross a cattleguard near some corrals. Continue across more small hills until you come to a T-intersection. Turn right on FS 67 and go up the hill.

Over the next 0.5 mile you pass two roads leading off to your right; don't take either one. Pass through a small grove of pine trees and head down the bigger hill. Just past the grove the road makes a slight fork; veer to the right. If you look north across the canyon from here, you will see the road that leads out of the gulch. You will know if you have taken all the correct turns if the road you are on veers to the right as it drops into the canyon. If you have taken a wrong turn, the road will veer to the left as it descends into the canyon.

Cross American Gulch at the bottom of this steep hill (5.8 miles). This stream flows year-round, fed partly by treated wastewater from Payson, and partly by runoff from the town of Payson itself. There are some native fish in this stream and you can take a minute to look for them. Be careful at this crossing. The water levels can be quite high, especially after a storm.

Just across the creek there is a road that turns downstream; don't take that one. The road you want goes uphill and more or less straight ahead. Climb this steep and rocky hill, taking a couple of switchbacks. After about 0.5 mile you will climb out of the canyon and the road becomes easier.

You pass a stock tank off to the left called White Tank, and at the top of the hill you meet a four-way intersection (6.1 miles). The road to your left leads down to the East Verde River and the Gowan Mine. It is a very steep, dead-end ride. The road to the right leads up the hill, where you want to be going.

(You can add about 1.5 miles to your ride by following the road straight ahead. It drops into the canyon and crosses it. When you come to another four-way intersection, take the road to the right up the steep hill. The other two routes are dead-ends that take you down to the river. Follow your road up the steep hill to White Mountain and White Mountain Mine. From the mine the trail will come off the mountain, crossing two small wash canyons before climbing back up to meet the main trail.)

The main route continues up the steepening hill. You get one little break in climbing, a short downhill section that drops you into the side of Summit Canyon. The climb resumes here and takes on some really hideous proportions. It is relentlessly steep, with some pitches of 45 degrees crossing over loose and sliding rock. There is plenty of pushing here, but if you want to feel better, stop and look at the spectacular views behind you to the west. Across the canyon to your right you can see the buildings of the Summit Mine.

Once you reach the top of the ridge, turn right and follow the road back toward the town, which you can see clearly from here. This is the edge of Birch Mesa. There are a couple of jeep trails on the top of this ridge, but you'll find your way if you just stick to the main trail (they all let out in more or less the same spot anyway). When you come to a nicely maintained gravel road, turn left. This is the road to the Summit Mine.

After a few feet, you cross a cattleguard and meet a paved road (8.8 miles). Turn right and follow this road about 0.25 mile through an L bend to your left. Bomb down this hill to where it intersects Vista. Turn right on Vista Road, follow it to the end of the mesa, and then dive down the steep, smooth tarmac. There are no surprise turns here so you can open it wide up.

Follow the road past the cemetery and across the golf course.

Notes

At the end of the golf course is the wastewater treatment plant. This facility was constructed in 1972 and enlarged in 1983. Some of the treated water is used to water the golf course and the fields at Payson High School. The rest is pumped into the stream. Sludge dries downstream from the facility and is sold to farmers to use for fertilizer.

American Gulch is named after the American Flag Mine. Snowstorm Mountain got its name when someone discovered a mine prospect there during a snowstorm.

The Gowan Mine was established in 1878 and was the largest ore producer in the Payson mining district. It operated steadily through 1882. During the 1880s there were over 100 full-time miners in Payson, most of whom worked here. A 1918 mining report shows the remains of an old stamp mill still standing at the site.

The Summit Mine was established around the same time as the other mines near Payson. There was rarely enough water to run the

Stone entrance to the Payson Pioneer Cemetery.

Summit operation and it was never very profitable. In 1944 a field engineer reported that he did not think the mine was ever going to pay and recommended no further money be put into it. In 1948 the company offered 9,660 shares of stock for $5 a share, and a 1952 prospectus showed that they had earned $144,000 from the sale of stock and only $4,000 from the sale of ore and "other supplies." Their expenses totalled $147,810, leaving $190 in the bank.

Birch Mesa was named by William Burch who owned a ranch near some springs at the base of this hill. Burch came to Payson in 1876. He worked as a miner and started the first sawmill in the area before he married Ida Hazelton in 1883. They started ranching and William worked as a sheriff's deputy and Justice of the Peace from 1891 to 1893, when he and his family moved from Payson. Over the years Burch's name was misspelled on different maps, and the official name of the mesa is a misspelling of the original.

4. Round Valley

Highlights: Tests your hills abilities
Seasons: All year, hot in summer
Distance: 7.9 miles
Time: 2 hours
Difficulty Rating: Moderate
High Elevation: 5,200 feet   **Low Elevation:** 4,800 feet
USGS Topographic Maps: Payson South
Access: Head 3 miles south on Arizona 87 to the Round Valley turnoff.
Turn east into Round Valley. Turn left at the intersection marked "upper and lower Round Valley" (you want lower). After about 1 mile you
will meet some houses and a "Flash Flood Warning" sign (1.3 miles
from the intersection). On your left are two houses with chainlink
fences around the front yards. The road you want is a few yards past
these houses to the left. Park on the dirt here.

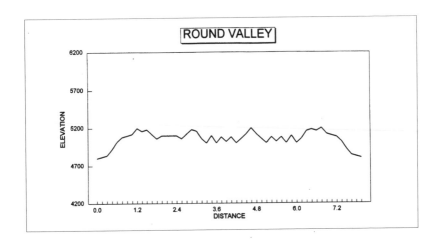

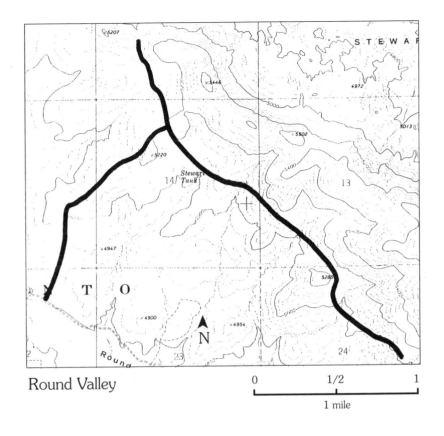

Round Valley

```
0          1/2          1
├──────────┴──────────┤
        1 mile
```

The Route

At the start of this ride there are a number of intersecting roads, as this is a popular four-wheeler area, but they all get you to the same spot. The roads are dirt and mud, but soon change to rocky, steep climbing trails (0.4 mile).

At the top of the hill the trail levels off a bit (0.8 mile), then continues up, at times nearly level and at other times fairly steep. Follow a slight downhill to a T in the road. Turn left. Drop into a wash and then head up the hill on the other side, climbing up to a saddle (2.2 miles). From the saddle you can see the Rim and parts of Payson. The trail continues steeply down the pass from this side and into Payson.

Legend has it that this was the old wagon road between Payson and Round Valley. Unfortunately, the trail crosses private land and you cannot ride your bike all the way to town from here. This is a good spot to turn around.

When you get back to the intersection (2.9 miles) go straight. The road climbs for a bit and then drops steeply into a wash. For the next 1.8 miles the road is very steep and rocky. You will climb up ridges, then drop back down into washes.

At 4.6 miles you reach the high point of the ride. Stop to take a good look at the valley. The trail continues on for another 0.7 mile past here, but it is more of the same, so this is a good place to turn around.

Return by the same route, remembering to turn left at the T intersection (6.3 miles). From there, the descent is very fast, so be sure to watch for the rocky sections.

Notes

Round Valley was settled by Joseph and Ruth Gibson. They lived near the Virgin River in Utah before being called upon by the church to help settle Arizona. They first moved to Gisela and then to Round Valley in 1879. Ruth helped start the Round Valley School in 1881, the first in northern Gila County. The Gibsons had twelve children. Joe died in the late 1890s after his leg was crushed in an equestrian accident.

5. Oxbow Estates

Highlights: Nice introductory ride
Seasons: All year, hot in summer
Distance: 5.4 miles
Time: 2 hours
Difficulty Rating: Moderate
High Elevation: 4,820 feet   **Low Elevation:** 4,580 feet
USGS Topographic Maps: Payson South
Connecting Rides: 8. Marysville Hill
Access: Follow Arizona 87 south about 4 miles to the sign for Oxbow Estates on the west side of the road. Turn into Oxbow Estates. Follow the main road down about a quarter of a mile to the Walnut Street sign. Turn right here and follow the road up to North View Road. Turn right again and look for the jeep trail on your left (if you get to Trails West Road, you've gone too far). Park your car in the clearing at the start of the jeep trail.

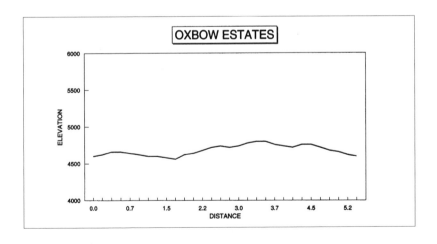

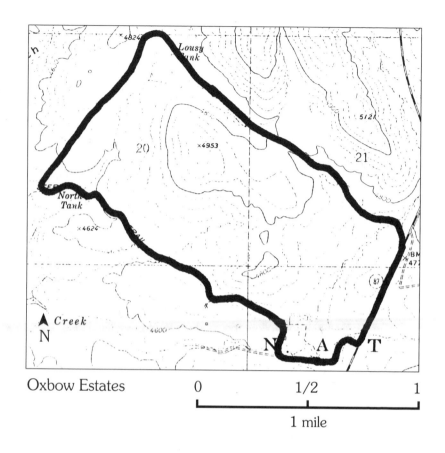

Oxbow Estates

0   1/2   1

1 mile

The Route

This ride starts out gently with a few little ups and downs. There are a couple of small wash crossings and ruts to keep it interesting.

After a short, gentle downhill you will come to a cattleguard at a fence line (1.3 miles). Cross the cattleguard, pass the trail immediately after the fence, and make a right turn on the next jeep trail to your right (1.4 miles). This trail generally trends upward with a number of short, somewhat rocky hills. When you reach an intersection, turn right onto the well-defined road (2.4 miles).

Continue on through a gate (2.5 miles), up the hill, and pass through another gate (2.8 miles). This road will take you up and over a saddle and then send you downhill to the mine area. Turn right at the mine (3.7 miles) and climb up to the highway. If you want the easy road back to Oxbow Estates, take the highway and cruise south down the wide shoulder.

If you are up for more adventure, turn onto the road to your right just before you pass under the mine company sign. This road follows the powerlines up a small hill and down the other side. This side is fairly steep and rocky and is a good place to test your downhill ability. Follow the powerlines back to Oxbow Estates Road and turn right.

Notes

Oxbow Estates is located on the north side of Oxbow Hill. In 1871 Charles B. Genung was traveling through here with several troops. Their guide warned them that the Apache on the south side of the hill were likely to attack so they came up the hill on the north side, hoping to avoid the tribe. Despite their precautions the Apache set fire to the range, scattering the troops and forcing them to find another way into Payson.

The first settler here was William O. St. John who helped find the Oxbow Mine in 1878. He raised dairy cows and five thousand goats on the ranch, despite the constant attacks of coyotes on his livestock. His ranch, known as St. Johns Place, was on the original road to Payson and was a favorite stopping place, as horses could drink their fill at the spring on the ranch. William and his wife operated a post office and general store on the ranch as well. Each fall William would head to Payson to kill a wagon load of deer. He would make jerky from the meat to help feed the miners at the Oxbow Mine.

About fifty *mano-y-metates*, American Indian grinding tools, have been found in the wash southeast of the property. Prehistoric inhabitants probably farmed corn at the springs.

MINING COUNTRY

The word to describe the mining country is *BIG*. Big hills, big canyons, big dreams, and stunning vistas. This is the only area of the Rim Country with true Sonoran desert vegetation. There is a vast grove of Arizona Cypress trees, but most of the mining country is desert: hot days, cool nights, little water, and thorny cactus. Some of the canyons that have permanent water sport thick, lush riparian vegetation.

This is the only area of the Rim Country that has had productive mines. Most of the mines were located during the 1880s and have operated on and off since then. Very few were ever economically viable, but they served to help bring in settlers.

Some mining sites have been worked recently, but the Arizona Department of Mines and Minerals lists no working mines near Payson in its 1994 report. Look for abandoned machinery, cars, and shacks. Be careful of mine tunnels and shafts. Never enter them—they can collapse at any given moment. A Payson man died in 1994 after falling into a ninety-foot shaft. The environmental damage caused by unreclaimed mining activities is readily apparent at many mine sites.

6. Cypress Thicket

Highlights: Cypress Thicket, Table Mountain, Excursion Mine
Seasons: All year; very hot and dry in summer months
Distance: 17.6 miles
Time: 6 hours
Difficulty Rating: Strenuous
High Elevation: 4,977 feet   **Low Elevation:** 3,600 feet
USGS Topographic Maps: Payson South, North Peak
Connecting Rides: 2. Peach Orchard Springs, 3. Snowstorm Mountain,
7. Doll Baby Ranch, 8. Marysville Hill, 10. Wild Rye Creek,
11. Table Mountain
Access: Head south about 1 mile to the intersection of Arizona 87 and
Main Street. Follow Main Street 1 mile west through downtown to the
Museum of the Forest. Park at the museum.

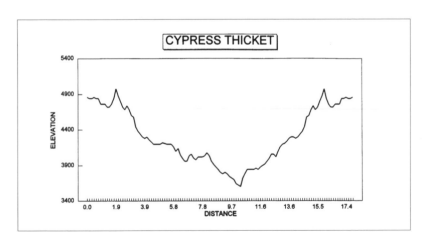

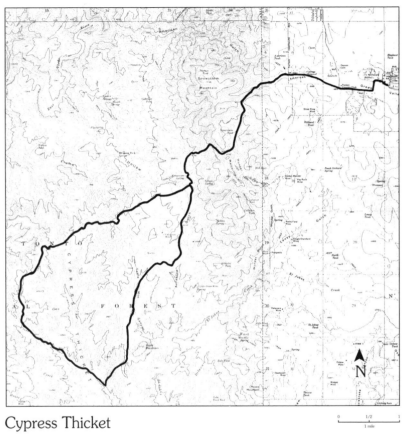

Cypress Thicket

0   1/2   1
1 mile

N

The Route

Follow Main Street west from the museum, passing Julia Randall Elementary School and the Payson Country Club and onto the dirt road straight ahead. After about 200 yards you will pass the entrance to the sewage treatment plant and come to the American Gulch. Follow the gulch, crossing the stream twice.

The route climbs up the hill to your left as the American Gulch swings away to the north. Climb this steep hill and follow the main road through the low, sometimes muddy area and then over another small hill. (There are a couple of smaller roads in this area, but stick to the main route.) The road drops away quickly from this point and is fairly steep and rocky.

You meet the road to Cypress Thicket (3.3 miles). Turn left and keep to the left at the small intersection as soon as you turn. You will come quickly to two concrete water crossings, first at Grapevine and then at Grimes Springs. Just after coming out of the wash, turn right onto FS 414.

The next 2.5 miles will give you some of the best downhill experiences of your life. The road follows the ridge line down, at first gently and then more and more steeply. The vegetation is somewhat sparse when you first turn onto this road, but becomes increasingly dense as you descend. This is the Cypress Thicket. You will notice that the trees grow thicker on the south sides of the hills than on the north sides.

Continue straight after passing through a gate where the road descends even more steeply. Look out for veins of harder rock that run through the road as you go down—they can get you airborne easily.

The road climbs out of a steep-sided wash and over a solid outcropping of white rock. At the top of this hill is a road to your right (7.6 miles) that eventually leads to Pole Hollow Spring and the head of Pole Hollow Canyon. Veer to the left and continue on the main road.

Climb another short steep hill past a road to your right. You will meet a signed road in another 100 yards, down a steep hill (8.2 miles). The sign for Cypress Thicket and North Peak Trailhead points to your right. Turn left.

Continue to follow the main road to your left, passing a small road on your right. The route crosses a wash and a couple of sandy areas as it descends. After you cross a cattleguard, look for FS 193 (10.3 miles). Turn left on FS 193 and climb up the steep hill. This section of the road is seriously eroded.

At the top of the hill is an intersection. Turn toward your left, where Table Mountain is clearly visible. Keep to your left as you climb up to the backbone of Table Mountain.

When you come to an intersection beyond Table Mountain, again continue to your left (11.5 miles). Cross two cattleguards and follow the fence line up toward Marysville Hill. You will drop into Table Mountain Canyon, crossing the creek three times.

Climb out of the canyon to an intersection on top of the hill. Turn right and head down into Arrastre Gulch and then climb immediately back up a big hill. Once you get to the top of this hill you will see the water tanks for the Excursion Mine. The mine is privately held and you are not allowed into the area. However, you can see a couple of old beat-up trailers that are used by the miners when they are here. Just past the mine (13.1 miles), continue to the right at the corral and intersection. This returns you to your original route.

Notes

Grapevine Spring was named in 1864 by King S. Woolsey, one of the first white visitors to the Rim Country. There were a number of grapevines growing at the spring that is located just upstream from the present crossing.

Grimes Canyon is named for an old prospector who had a cabin in this vicinity.

The Cypress Thicket gets its name from the Arizona Cypress tree, which grows in abundance there. This evergreen tree is sometimes grown for Christmas trees. Its strong wood was also used for fenceposts.

The Arrastre Gulch is actually a misspelling of the Spanish word *arrastra,* a term for a primitive ore-grinding mill. A huge flat granite rock was dragged, usually by a donkey, in a circle over a rock-lined pit filled with ore to be crushed. There were several of these contraptions in this drainage.

7. Doll Baby Ranch

Highlights: Many scenic vistas, Crackerjack Mine ruins, East Verde River

Seasons: All year, hot in summer; the route is impassible when the water is high after storms or during spring runoff

Distance: 29 miles

Time: All day

Difficulty Rating: Strenuous

High Elevation: 5,040 feet   **Low Elevation:** 3,400 feet

USGS Topographic Maps: Payson South, North Peak, Buckhead Mesa, and Payson North

Connecting Rides: 2. Peach Orchard Springs, 3. Snowstorm Mountain, 6. Cypress Thicket, 8. Marysville Hill, 14. Ash Creek Canyon, 18. Crackerjack

Access: Turn west on Overland Road at the intersection of Arizona 87 and Arizona 260 in Payson. Turn right on McLane Road, then left at Rumsey Park.

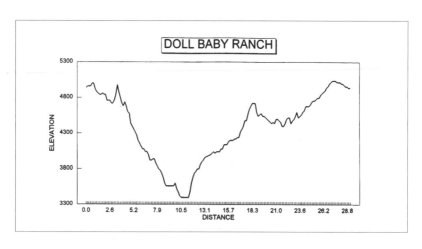

The Route

Leave Rumsey Park and turn south on McLane Road. Follow McLane south past Payson High School complex and up over the hill. The descent from this hill is steep with a stop sign at the bottom. Be careful here. Turn right on Main Street (1.1 miles).

Follow Main Street as it turns first left and then right along the golf course. The big hill across the golf course to your right is the site of Fort McDonald. This is the only place from which you get a clear view of the fort site while on the rides described in this book. The fort figures prominently in the early history of the town.

Just past the golf course the road turns to dirt. Look for the mileage sign. You are now on FS 406. Follow the dirt road past the sewage treatment plant and sludge drying beds, crossing the stream twice.

As the gulch swings away to the north, stay on the road as it climbs steeply straight ahead. The descent from the top of this hill is steep, loose, and rocky. The route in this small basin can also be rutted, especially in the spring. Follow the main road through this section and disregard the few side roads you pass here. Make a short ascent to the top of the next hill, Marysville Hill (4.3 miles).

The descent from Marysville Hill is very steep, rutted, and rocky. After passing a cattleguard you will come to an intersection where the road to the left leads to Cypress Thicket (4.9 miles). Stay to the right and keep to the main road for the next several miles.

After you cross a cattleguard and enter into Simonton Flat (9.0 miles), you are on private land that is part of the Doll Baby Ranch. The ranch sits in the river bottom not too far from here. Climb the hill after the flat and note the ranch outbuildings to your right.

After a U-turn, there is a very steep descent into City Creek (9.8 miles). At the bottom of the canyon is the trailhead for the City Creek Trail, which leads up into the wilderness area. (No bikes are allowed on this trail because the wilderness boundary has not yet been established.)

Cross the rocky creek bottom at the old windmill. You are now at the section of Doll Baby Ranch in the East Verde River Canyon (10.6 miles). The road takes you into an area of lush vegetation, with many vines and large cottonwood and sycamore trees.

After a short, slightly downhill run, cross through a fence and

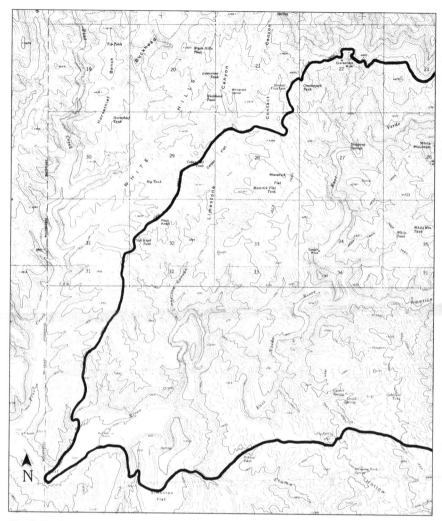

Doll Baby Ranch

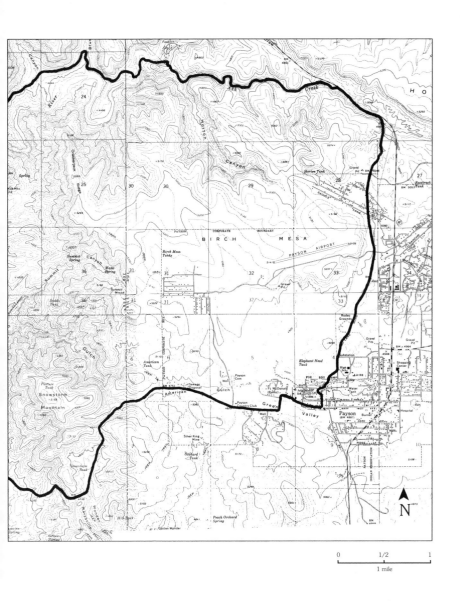

continue straight ahead (11.4 miles). Turn right at the new road and cross the East Verde River. *Do not attempt to cross the river if it is more than knee-deep. The currents can be very strong in this river.* The new road climbs gently up the canyon wall about 200 yards before it turns left up the steeper hill. A short distance after the road tops out of the canyon, you will pass through a large range gate in an area thick with mesquite trees (12.5 miles). Another mile of climbing and a short downhill bring you to a second gate (13.7 miles). There are a number of century plants here.

From this point, soil is mercifully interspersed with the rocky road. There is a steep rocky section where you will need to push (15.9 miles). At the top of this section you'll find a mass of smooth dark gray rock. This is limestone.

At the top of this hill you will cross through areas of grassland mixed with juniper and piñon pine forests. Continue up the hill as it gets steeper and steeper until you come to a signed Forest Service intersection (17.7 miles). Take a right here and continue up the steep hill. The road to your left, FS 209, leads out to Arizona 87.

From the top of this hill you have good views of the surrounding mountains (18.5 miles). To your right is a pile of mine tailings and two deep mine shafts. Do not get too close to these shafts as they may cave in without warning. There are several jeep trails in this area. Be sure to stick to the main road. You may have to walk your bike down this steep and rocky hill until you get to what is left of Crackerjack Mine (19.0 miles), where the road smooths out.

As you traverse along the side of the mountain you will begin to see glimpses of the East Verde River off to your right. Look closely and you will see a fairly good-sized waterfall. There is a jeep trail that leads down to the river here (20.2 miles).

The road continues to contour around the side of the hill and then drops suddenly into Brushy Canyon, which is full of sycamore and cottonwood trees. There may be running water in the creek bed. Where this canyon joins the East Verde Canyon, the river is close and a couple of jeep trails lead down to the water.

The road climbs over a saddle where the river makes a large bend to the south, then drops back down to a concrete crossing (22.6 miles). This is an excellent wading pool.

As you come out of the river bottom you can see the houses at East Verde Park. To your left is a road blocked by a large gate leading into the development (23.1 miles). Continue straight.

Continue up and over the saddle underneath the power lines. After the saddle the route drops into picturesque Ash Creek Canyon, then climbs upstream. There are a number of water crossings as you climb. After about 1 mile the canyon widens. There are log fences to keep people from tearing up the fragile meadows. Follow this road on to Arizona 87 (25.9 miles). Make a right turn and follow the highway up the hill about 0.5 mile until you come to another dirt road to your right. Take this road back into the forest, where you will climb up some fairly rocky sections.

Continue straight ahead at the four-way intersection (27.4 miles). Thread your way through the boulder roadblock and back onto the paved road. You are now on McLane Road again. Follow this road straight ahead for about 2 miles back down to Rumsey Park.

Notes

Fort McDonald was probably named after William McDonald who came to Payson in 1878. He homesteaded a ranch north of the fort hill and built his cabin at the top. During conflicts with Apache in 1881 and 1882, the residents of Payson and Marysville set up defenses at his cabin. After that, the hill became known as Fort McDonald.

The Mazatzal Mountains are visible for a large portion of this ride. *Mazatzal* is an Apache word meaning bleak or barren. There was a small Mormon settlement in City Canyon in the late 1870s called Mazatzal City. The town was abandoned in 1882 when the Mormons moved to Pine.

The Doll Baby Ranch was started by Napoleon Bonaparte Chilson in 1882 when the Mormons left the area. People had a hard time with his long name, so they nicknamed him "Poley." He ran cattle on the mesa to the west of the ranch, Polle's Mesa. Baby Doll Ranch was named in 1906 by George Smith, but the name has been turned around over the years. The ranch has never had telephone or electric service. The current owners run about 150 head of cattle. Additions to the original wooden house have been built over the years and it now serves as the main ranch building, which you can see from the road.

Notice the park-like setting to your right in the river's floodplain. If you look at the upstream side of the trees, you will see stacks of debris deposited by periodic floods.

The first European to see this country was Antoine Leroux, who was guiding an expedition led by Lieutenant Whipple in 1854. Leroux used the river as a route to get from the lower deserts, around what is now Phoenix, to the top of the Rim. In 1864 "King" Woolsey used the river to travel from the top of the Rim down to the Verde River. He named the river the East Fork of the Verde.

The Crackerjack Mine operated off and on over the years since it was discovered in the 1880s. One of the biggest problems miners faced was the poor road leading to it. It was worked for a while during World War II, and the last record of any improvements there is from 1977.

8. Marysville Hill

Highlights: Numerous mines, some single-track trail

Seasons: All year, hot in summer

Distance : 9.1 miles

Time: 3 hours

Difficulty Rating: Moderate

High Elevation: 4,920 feet   **Low Elevation:** 4,340 feet

USGS Topographic Maps: Payson South and North Peak

Connecting Rides: 2. Peach Orchard Springs, 3. Snowstorm Mountain, 5. Oxbow Estates, 6. Cypress Thicket, 7. Doll Baby Ranch

Access: Head south about 1 mile to the intersection of Arizona 87 and Main Street. Follow Main Street west through downtown to the Payson Country Club golf course, about 1.5 miles, and park.

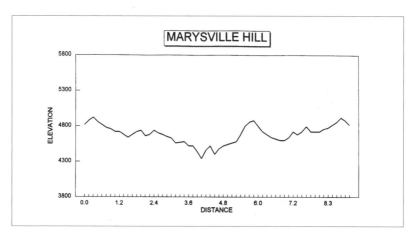

The Route

Head straight across the street from the country club toward a white house. What looks like a gravel driveway just to the east is

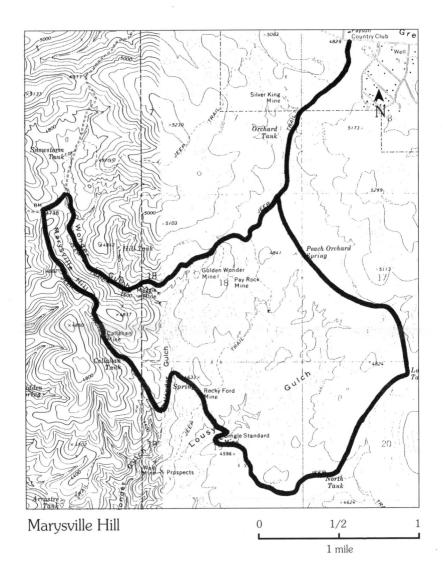

Marysville Hill

0   1/2   1

1 mile

actually the start of FS 441. Ride past the house and you will see the Forest Service gate; make sure you close the gate after you pass through.

Climb up this short hill to the saddle (0.3 mile). Descend down the main road and look for a trail that heads off to your left. It is fairly well-defined and breaks off through a manzanita thicket as the road swings away to the right (1.0 mile). Follow this single track down into and along the wash until you come to Peach Orchard Springs (1.3 miles).

Return to the road which is to your right as you come into the springs. Follow this well-maintained Forest Service road to your left (south). This road will carry you over some rolling hills until you come to a barbed wire fence to your left (2.4 miles). Take the rough jeep trail to your right here. If you come to a gate on the main road, you have gone too far.

Although rocky, this trail is a pleasant downhill. After 0.7 mile you will come to another well-maintained road (3.1 miles) that comes in from Oxbow Estates. Turn right and follow this road as it gently contours around the hill.

You will know when you get to Lousy Gulch because the road bombs down one side of the canyon and climbs straight up the other. A spring is at the bottom of the canyon (4.0 miles). This is the site of the Single Standard Mine. Once you get out of the steepest part of the canyon you will come to a saddle with several trails leading away from it (4.3 miles). Pay close attention here or you will get lost.

Straight up the hill ahead of you is a trail that used to lead to the Rocky Ford Mine. The main trail is just to the right of the mine access trail and climbs up and around the hill. Hard to your left, almost a U-turn, is another trail that gently climbs the hill behind you. *Do not take any of these trails.* The trail you want is the least well-defined of all of the trails here and it descends into the brush to your left.

Drop down this single track into a thicket of trees (4.5 miles). The trail seems to dead-end at the tiny springs, but it does not. Behind you and to your left, across the water, the trail climbs out of the creek bed up onto a hill.

When you get to the ridge look for a trail leading up the ridge to your right (4.7 miles). Do not take the better-looking trail that continues on around the ridge down into a wash. The trail you are looking for will look like a washed-out mining prospect. Once you get past the washed-out section, the trail is fairly well-defined.

Continue up the ridge and follow the trail as it drops into a wash. The trail is indistinct here, but it generally follows the wash. You will come to a large mound of dirt in the middle of the wash. Push your bike up to the top of this mound (5.1 miles). This used to be Callahan Tank, which was built to help supply water to the Callahan Mine.

Approaching Lousy Gulch on the Marysville Hill ride.

Because the mining operation, just upstream from here, caused a lot of erosion, the tank filled in with dirt and now appears to be just a dirt flat. Follow the trail around the former tank to the right, until you come to another dirt mound (5.2 miles). At the top of this mound is the site of Callahan Mine. You will find old mining equipment here as well as a couple of partially caved-in mine tunnels and shafts. Please do not go in any of them!

The trail heads up the hill to your right. It is very steep and rocky and will require some pushing. Near the top of the hill is a chain gate. Just past the gate is a saddle with several trails (5.5 miles). Take the trail hard to your left. From the saddle you can see the large Golden Wonder Mine to the east. You will pass by it in a little bit.

The trail climbs up to the top of Marysville Hill before dropping back down to well-maintained Forest Service Road 406 at another saddle (6.1 miles). Turn right here. Drop quickly to another intersection (6.3 miles). Turn right at the large sign that says you are on FS 441 and that Peach Orchard Springs is 2 miles away and Highway 87 is 6 miles away.

Follow this road down the wash. Soon you will meet a fork with one branch leading down into the wash and the other climbing up the hill to your left (6.8 miles). Turn left. This road will take you around the hill past the Golden Wonder Mine. Stay to the left at the mine.

The Golden Wonder is the largest mine you will see on this trip. Note the extensive damage to the area and the large portion of the hill that has been cut away. There is also a shabby mobile home here that miners use when they are working the area. Climb the steep road as it passes the mine up and over the hill. Descend the other side until you come to a four-way intersection (7.8 miles). Take the left-hand turn.

After a bit, you will pass the trail you turned down earlier to get into Peach Orchard Springs. Follow the main road to the left, up and over the saddle. Drop back down to the fence, and you are back to the country club.

Notes

In the 1870s miners began working the area around the present-day golf course. The main mine here was the Golden Waif and it operated from 1875 to 1890. Although hundreds of mining claims were made during those years, very few of them made any money. In fact, the Payson mining district was a rather poor one.

Lousy Gulch got its name from Ben Cole and his sons, Elmer and Link, who worked as miners here in the winter of 1880. They all picked up severe cases of lice.

The Golden Wonder Mine has an interesting history. It was originally located in 1877 but was never worked extensively. In 1980, the Arizona Corporation Commission accused the two mining companies running the claim of fraud. The companies had sold $40,000 in unregistered securities to investors, claiming that the mine was on the brink of paying off. The company owners told investors that they owned a dozen mining properties when in fact they owned only two. They also showed investors mining equipment at the site, but failed to tell them that the equipment was borrowed. Investors were told that they would double or triple their money, and one gentleman was told that he would make $65,000 on his $1,000 investment. It turns out the money was being used to pay off old debts and to purchase mining equipment registered in the mine owners' names, not the company's. After a day-long hearing in April of 1980, the mine owners were absolved of any wrongdoing. A 1987 feasibility study concluded that the mine was not likely to be profitable because it had shown a poor recovery rate.

Marysville was established in 1880 to service the mines in the area, and Elmer Chilson opened a store here in 1881. One story claims that Chilson named the town "Marysville" in honor of his six-year-old daughter. Another story claims that the town was named for Mary Pyeatt who settled a couple of miles west of here, toward the Doll Baby Ranch. If the latter story is true, then the town actually may have been named for Mary's five-year-old daughter Mary, who died a year before the town was settled. The town existed about three years until the main settlement area moved into the Big Green Valley (present-day Payson).

9. Oxbow Hill

Highlights: Thrilling descent
Seasons: All year, hot in summer
Distance: 11 miles
Time: 3 hours
Difficulty Rating: Difficult
High Elevation: 4,720 feet   **Low Elevation:** 3,120 feet
USGS Topographic Maps: Payson South, Gisela
Connecting Rides: 10. Wild Rye Creek, 11. Table Mountain
Access: Head 5 miles south on Arizona 87. Look for FS 537 to your right just after Oxbow Estates and just before the safety pullout.

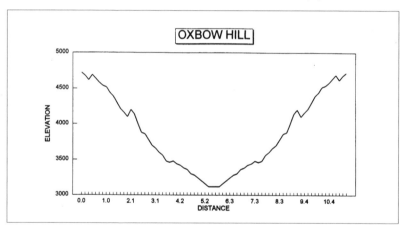

The Route

Two trails leave from where you are parked; both are marked. Begin this ride on FS 537, the trail to the left (south).

The road immediately descends into a small wash and climbs out the other side. The main road turns downhill to your left and descends

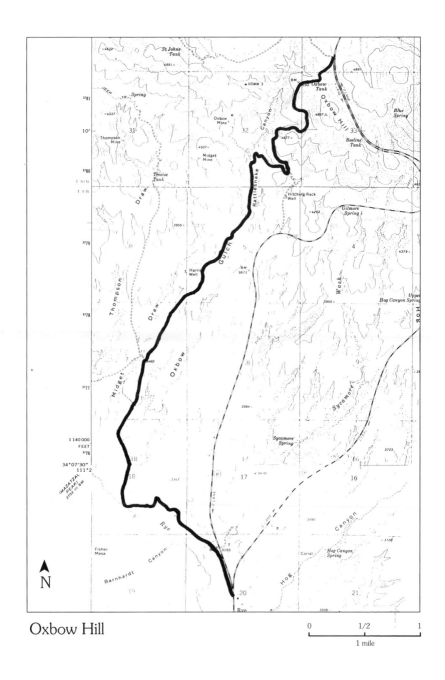

Oxbow Hill

0   1/2   1

1 mile

sharply. Be careful on this descent as there is little "run out": the road just keeps going down with very little change to help slow your speed.

The road contours around the side of Oxbow Hill as it descends into Rattlesnake Canyon. The views from this section are spectacular if you can peel your eyes off the road long enough to look.

You will come to a T-intersection (1.6 miles). Turn right and descend to the bottom of Rattlesnake Canyon. Climb steeply out the other side.

Once you get out of the canyon there is an old water tank in the flat area (2.1 miles). If you look up the road to the right, you will see the remains of the Oxbow Mine up on the hill. Turn left here, where there is a nice view of the town of Rye and Highway 87.

At mile 2.5 you will come to a small intersection. Both roads will take you to the same location. To your right are the remains of a mine in the bottom of the wash and to your left is a big cottonwood tree that offers shade if you need it.

Once you get out of this wash continue down the hill. Pass a small road off to your right and continue straight ahead. The road levels off slightly and is not quite so rocky here, so you can turn up your speed if you want to. Off to your right is the Harris Well windmill.

Once you come to a large intersection on a nice road (3.6 miles), take a left down FS 414. The road is much smoother now and not nearly so steep. In fact, there are a couple of small uphills, but nothing to slow you down too much.

Cruise down the road and notice the large cottonwood trees in the creek bottom at the Last Roundup Ranch. This road finally dumps you out on the frontage road, across the highway from the Rye Bar (5.5 miles). This is a good place to stop for refreshments and, if you've arranged it, to call your ride to come pick you up. If not, turn around and grind back up the hill to your car, about two hours away.

Notes

In 1871 Charles B. Genung and a group of soldiers discovered several ox yokes near the base of Oxbow Hill. Apparently, American Indians had stolen the oxen still in their yokes and stopped here to take the yokes off. Genung named it Ox Yoke Hill.

Several years later the Oxbow Mine was developed high on the mountain on the south side. A small town was established downhill from the mine and a post office operated there from 1894 to 1908. Oxbow Hill was an obstacle for wagon freighters bringing goods from Globe to Payson because the route was so long and steep. Freighters leading more than one wagon were forced to unhitch them and haul them up the mountain one at a time. They would then reassemble their team for the final haul into Payson. While you are riding back up this trail, you can imagine what drudgery they must have felt.

 # 10. Wild Rye Creek

Highlights: Cypress Thicket
Seasons: All year, hot in summer
Distance: 17.7 miles
Time: 6 hours
Difficulty Rating: Difficult
High Elevation: 4,040 feet   **Low Elevation:** 3,120 feet
USGS Topographic Maps: Gisela, Payson South, North Peak
Connecting Rides: 6. Cypress Thicket, 9. Oxbow Hill, 11. Table Mountain
Access: Follow Arizona 87 south to Rye, about 13 miles. Park at the Rye Bar.

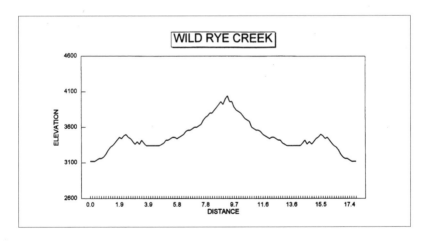

The Route

From Rye Bar, cross Arizona 87 to the west and turn right on the access road. After a few yards the road turns to dirt. Follow it straight

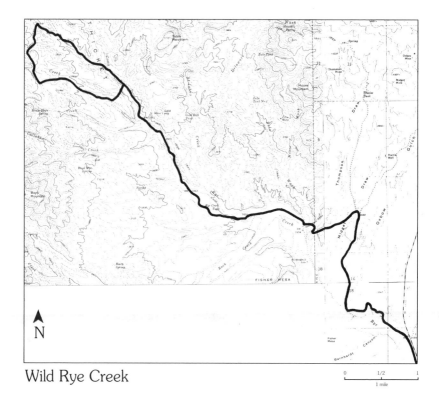

Wild Rye Creek

0   1/2   1
1 mile

ahead past the ranch in the creek bottom to your left. Follow the gravel road over a couple of small hills until you get to the signed intersection of FS 414 and FS 537 (2.3 miles). Take FS 414 to your left and head down into the bottom of Rye Creek.

You will meet a couple of roads here. The best road, to your right, leads to Zulu Mine. The road hard to your left leads across the creek to a windmill. Take the other road to the left that leads down into the creek bottom. Unless someone has shot the sign down, the road is marked FS 414.

This is a pleasant ride; there are huge sycamore and cottonwood trees that shade the road. Over the next several miles, the road climbs steadily, sometimes steeply, crossing the wash several times. It becomes steeper as you get closer to the mountains.

Follow the main road (FS 414) straight ahead, past the signed intersection for FS 193 to your right (6.9 miles). About 1.5 miles past that intersection, look for the first jeep trail to your left (7.4 miles). It is hard to see, but it is just 200 or so yards this side of the Cypress Thicket sign. If you get to the sign, you have gone too far.

Once you locate the trail, take it across the wash and up the hill. This route is easy to follow as it goes over a couple of hills. Ignore the roads you pass that lead uphill to the right.

When you get to the corrals, the main road looks as though it turns uphill to the right. Go around the corrals and look for the somewhat overgrown road that descends down the hill.

The descent from the corral is fast and smooth. The trail is free of ruts so you can "let it fly." The road follows the ridge line, then crosses the wash bottom, and takes you back to FS 414 (10.8 miles). Turn right here.

You can "power-pedal" as you come down FS 414. The road is not steep so you will need to pedal, but it is steep enough that you won't lose momentum. You don't have any climbs until you get down near Rye, but these are not too steep and they won't slow you down much.

Notes

The town of Rye was established at a popular crossing of Rye Creek. A former election precinct here was called Wild Rye because of the wild rye plants that grow along the creek banks.

A school opened in Rye in 1883, and the Haught family moved here from higher in the Rim Country in 1898. Their ranch would eventually grow to about ten thousand head of cattle and one thousand horses.

11. Table Mountain

Highlights: Trezise Tank, Table Mountain
Seasons: All year, hot in summer
Distance: 17.3 miles
Time: All day
Difficulty Rating: Strenuous
High Elevation: 4,240 feet   **Low Elevation:** 3,120 feet
USGS Topographic Maps: Gisela, Payson South, North Peak
Connecting Rides: 6. Cypress Thicket, 9. Oxbow Hill, 10. Wild Rye Creek
Access: Follow Arizona 87 south to Rye, about 13 miles. Park at the Rye Bar.

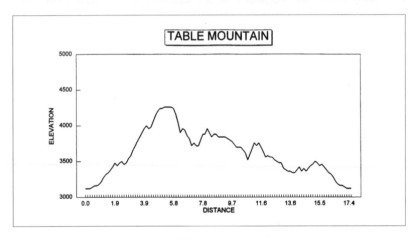

The Route

From Rye Bar, cross Arizona 87 to the west and turn right on the access road. After a few yards the road turns to dirt. Follow it straight ahead past the ranch in the creek bottom to your left.

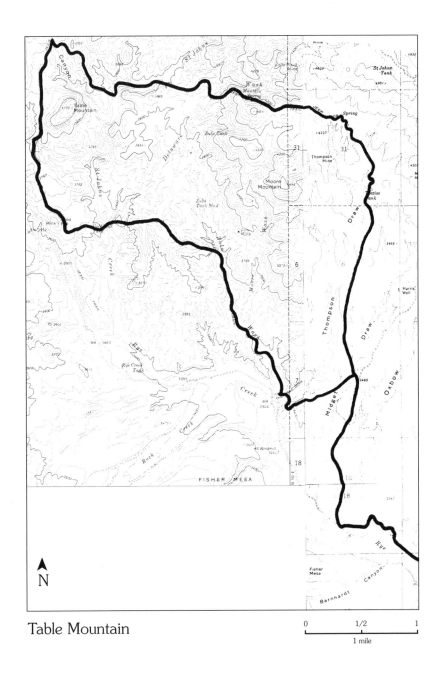

Table Mountain

Go over a couple of small hills until you get to the signed intersection of FS 414 and FS 537 (2.3 miles). Take FS 414 to the left and then take the jeep trail that leads to your right just a few feet beyond the crest of the hill.

Follow this trail across the small wash and then up the hill. Stick to the main trail and ignore the couple of minor trails you pass as you climb.

Descend into a lush area thick with cottonwood trees and surrounded by a barbed wire fence. Here you will see Trezise Tank (4.1 miles).

Follow the road around the side of the tank and up again. It will crest the ridge and level out. The wreckage of two old pickup trucks marks the intersection of a small road. Stay to the left and avoid the steep trail to the right. At one time there was a ranch here; the small corral is still used. Continue past the corral and head for the hill directly ahead. Pass the trail to the right that leads to Delaware Mine and the trail to the left that leads up Moore Mountain. Continue straight ahead on the main road. Be careful as the area can be a bit confusing.

The road you want descends the hill straight ahead of you on its north side. Table Mountain looms in the near distance. The descent is steep and rocky, but rideable. Partway down the hill there is a V in the road. Take the low road.

At the base of the hill you will come to a T-intersection (6.4 miles). If you are tired of climbing you can save yourself 4.2 miles of the total ride by turning to the left and climbing the hill. (Just on the other side is Zulu Mine, where you can rejoin the longer ride described below. You may have to pick your way down through the mine until you get to the road.)

The main route leads up the hill to the right. Just over the top of the hill the road splits. Take the right turn. If you come to a range gate, you have taken the wrong trail. The trail you want drops down quickly to St. Johns Creek. The large stand of pine trees at the creek is a refreshing place to stop. A recent mine claim has been made here, so be careful not to disturb anything.

Once you get to the creek bottom there is a road that leads out of the canyon to your right. Do not take this road. Take the jeep trail that leads down into the wash. This trail follows the wash for a while, sometimes in the wash and sometimes on the bank to the right.

Just past a narrow section the creek turns sharply away from the trail that you will follow to the right (7.6 miles). There are a couple of good wading pools here. The trail heads more or less straight up the steep hill. The route is somewhat overgrown, but it is not too difficult to find. You will probably have to push up a couple of the steeper sections.

The road levels out a bit as it contours around the side of the hill. Follow it until you meet a rusted iron gate. Go through this gate and descend into the wash. On the other side of the wash, take FS 193 (8.5 miles) to the left.

Climb a little bit and then begin a long, smooth descent. Around on the south side of Table Mountain the road splits again (9.5 miles). If you are tired of climbing and ready for an easy coast most of the rest of the way back, take the road to your right. After 0.3 mile you will reach FS 414 and can take it back to Rye Bar. If you want to continue, take the road to the left.

This route descends and then climbs the knoll known as Gold Hill. Climb up the north side of the hill before descending straight into a former stock tank labelled "Gold Hill Tank" on the map. Follow the road through the tank and out the other side, where it descends another steep hill.

At the bottom of the hill take the turn to the left. This is where most of the motorized traffic goes, so it won't be too hard to find. The road descends into the small but impressive St. Johns Canyon. Cross the canyon and continue on up the hill. This climb is somewhat rolling with occasional flats and descents. Once you top out on the hill, you will begin a quick descent down to Zulu Mine (12 miles). Cross over the cattleguard and through the gate. Turn right and head down the hill. You can see the Zulu Mine buildings off to your left.

The road is graded and covered with gravel. At the bottom of the hill you will meet the intersection of FS 414 (13.2 miles). Take FS 414 to the east over several small, rolling hills back into Rye.

Notes

This ride is located in an area once frequented by a man named Sam Hill. He came into Arizona in 1869 to prospect and he made several mining claims here. In 1872 he gave up mining to become head packer for the army in Arizona at a salary of $100 per month. He saw plenty of action with the army, but gave it up and returned to mining in 1880. He built a cabin near St. Johns Creek. Although he was involved with several mining ventures, he did not get rich from any of them. Like most of the mines in the Payson area, his did not pay off very well. He died of indigestion at the cabin of a man named Pat Walsh, with whom he had many mining claims.

The Oxbow Mine was started in 1876 by Al Sieber, William Moore, and William O. St. John and has operated sporadically throughout the twentieth century. In 1987 a Texas company worked up a detailed prospectus encouraging people to invest in "no risk" gold mining. Investors would pay $200 for 125 tons of raw ore, and an additional $1,800 to process it. The investor was to keep all the profits. In 1988 a securities group declined to invest in the operation because it could not track down the miners' references, had never heard of the lab that did the assay work, and found that the securities were not registered. The potential investors felt that investing in the gold mining operation would be like "touching leprosy." The record does not say what eventually transpired, but the Arizona Department of Mineral Resources' 1994 *Directory of Active Mines in Arizona* lists no active mines in the Payson area.

12. Royal Flush

Highlights: Spectacular views

Seasons: All year, hot in summer

Distance: 8.3 miles

Time: 2 hours

Difficulty Rating: Moderate

High Elevation: 5,000 feet   **Low Elevation:** 4,500 feet

USGS Topographic Maps: Payson South

Connecting Rides: 13. Gisela

Access: Head 4 miles south on Arizona 87. Look for the dirt road on the east side of the highway just past the Round Valley turnoff. Park your car at the entrance to FS 208.

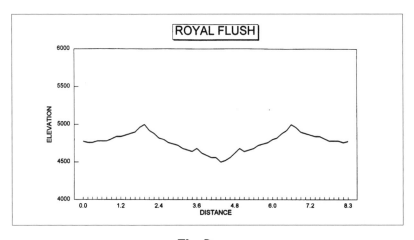

The Route

The road is easy to follow and climbs gently to a corral and windmill (1.2 miles). From here the road climbs more steeply and then

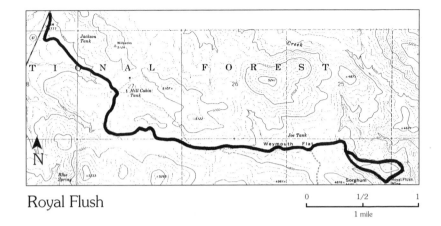

Royal Flush

```
0          1/2              1
|----------|----------|
        1 mile
```

descends to a shooting range (2.4 miles). This marks the end of the good road.

Continue straight ahead down the hill. The first part of this section looks a little scary, but the road actually eases up a bit and you can descend without your brakes—just watch for gullies and ruts across the road.

Cross the cattleguard and continue straight ahead. Ignore the small trails off to your left and continue straight along the clearly defined road. You will pass by the turnoff for the descent to Gisela (3.3 miles).

At 3.7 miles there is an intersection. Veer to the left here on what looks to be the high road. The road is in particularly good shape and lends itself to fast riding. (You will feel as though you are flying, no matter how fast you are going!) The scenery down the canyon to your left is spectacular while large powerlines lie directly in front of you, down in the canyon. This area is known as Hole-in-the-Ground. The hills beyond the canyon are part of the Hell's Gate Wilderness.

As you near the west end of the hill you will come to the remains of the Royal Flush Mine. Building foundations are clearly visible here, as is the main mine shaft down the road to your right. Follow this road to a four-way intersection. The road you will eventually take leads up to the right, but you may want to explore two other roads first.

The road to the left passes the old mine site and goes out to the edge of the hill a couple of yards beyond that. The road straight ahead

Mining Country

The wide, gentle road at the start of the Royal Flush ride.

leads down into the basin and dead-ends at the edge of the basin. It is a steep climb out, so be sure you are prepared for that before you plunge down the road.

To return, take the road to your right and follow it back to your car.

Notes

The Royal Flush was an undeveloped mine when a mining engineer visited it in the 1940s. It was worked more steadily in the 1960s and probably last operated in the early 1980s.

Hole-in-the-Ground is named for the large sinkhole at the canyon bottom.

13. Gisela

Highlights: Sonoran desert, canyon views

Seasons: All year, hot in summer

Distance: 19.2 miles

Time: All day

Difficulty Rating: Difficult

High Elevation: 5,000 feet   **Low Elevation:** 3,000 feet

USGS Topographic Maps: Payson South, Gisela

Connecting Rides: 12. Royal Flush

Access: Head 4 miles south on Arizona 87. Look for the dirt road on the east side of the highway just past the Round Valley turnoff. Park your car at the entrance to FS 208.

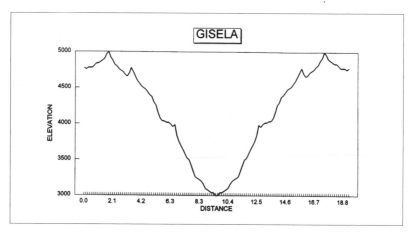

The Route

The road is easy to follow and climbs gently to a corral and windmill (1.2 miles). From here the road climbs more steeply and then descends to a shooting range (2.4 miles). This marks the end of the good road.

Continue straight down the hill. The first part of this section looks a little scary, but the road actually eases up a bit and you can descend without your brakes—just watch for gullies and ruts across the road.

Cross the cattleguard and continue straight ahead. Ignore the small trails off to your left and continue along the clearly defined road. Cross a second cattleguard and take the first Forest Service road to your right. This is the turnoff for Gisela (3.3 miles). Follow the road up and over the hill, to where the real downhill fun begins. This road is easy to follow, not too steep, and rocky only in spots. You can fly down this one. Just watch for the occasional rocky patches so that you can avoid a high-speed crash.

The road leads off to the right and descends into a drainage. As you head back out toward the edge of the hill, you will pass through a rutted area.

At mile 4.5, turn right across another cattleguard. (The road to the left goes uphill and ends with some extremely vertical stretches. Don't take that one.)

After a short stretch you will come upon a corral and another intersection (4.8 miles). Turn left. As you descend this section, Bishop Knoll rises up impressively before you.

Soon you will meet yet another intersection and corral (5.4 miles). Turn right and head down the steep, rocky wash. Off to your left you will see evidence of mining activity. The road levels out a bit at a low saddle. Avoid the trail that goes over the saddle, and continue down the main road underneath the powerlines (6.4 miles).

You will pass under the lines again at 6.6 miles, where the road begins to straighten out. If you pay attention in this area you will begin to see the saguaros of the Upper Sonoran Desert. The small town in the valley ahead of you is Gisela.

After a couple of steep switchbacks at the end of the hill (7.9 miles), the road twists into a canyon where it crosses a wash (8.2 miles). The road continues downhill and dives into a sandy wash (8.8 miles). There is not much road here; just follow the wash until you see the road again leading out of the wash to your right.

Head up the short hill, then down to the main dirt road (9.6 miles), which is about four lanes wide. This is a good place to turn around.

If you are adventurous, head down the main road to your right until you come to a sign that points to downtown Gisela. Here you'll find a large bar for liquid refreshments or thick steaks.

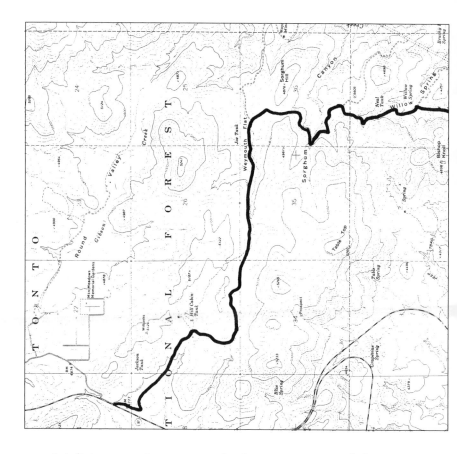

A left turn on the main road takes you to one of the nicest swimming holes in the state. It is up at The Narrows in Hell's Gate Wilderness, about 0.5 mile upstream on Tonto Creek. Park your bike where the road turns onto the private ranch. Barbed wire fence marks the Wilderness boundary at the mouth of impressive Houston Creek Canyon. Remember that bikes are prohibited in wilderness areas.

On your return trip you will see roads that V off from the route that you didn't notice when you were going 35 MPH downhill. Be sure to stick to the route you just traveled on the way out.

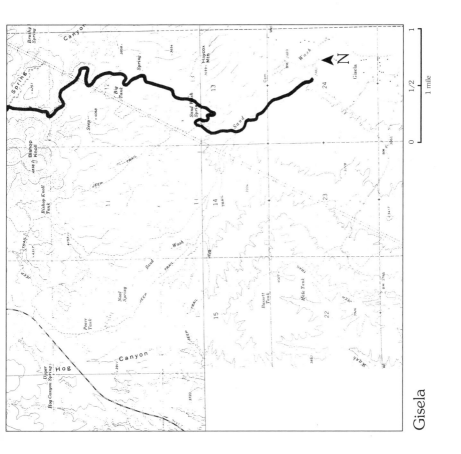

Gisela

Notes

Bishop Knoll is named for a young Mormon bishop who was in charge of Gisela.

Gisela was settled in 1881 by a Scotsman named David Gowan and his partner, Jim Samuels. The two men began by building an irrigation ditch. They dug in shifts, one working while the other kept watch for Apache marauders. Their work was stopped several times because of conflicts with the Apache, but they finally completed the ditch.

Gowan and Samuels brought sheep into the area. Buried in the wool of some of the sheep were seeds of a hardy forage grass, alfilaria. Known as "filaree," this grass was welcomed by area ranchers because it was a tender, early-spring addition to the local forage. Gowan and Samuels planted vegetables in their newly irrigated gardens as well as peach and apple trees. In 1882 Gowan left to settle at the Tonto Natural Bridge, and the Gisela property was sold to Mort and John Sanders. Cornelius Jackson bought the place in 1890 and encouraged his daughter and her husband to move their family to Gisela. Ellen Jackson Neal and William Neal, a former Texas Ranger, moved their family from Globe, Arizona, to Gisela in 1891. They raised goats primarily because they had seen so much trouble over cattle in the Pleasant Valley War, but they did run a small herd of cattle.

Mrs. Stanton, the local schoolteacher and wife of the future postmaster, suggested the town be named Gisela after the heroine in the novel *Countess Gisela*. The post office was opened in 1894.

In 1905 William Neal drowned while trying to cross the flooded Tonto Creek. He was trying to check on his goats that were penned up on the other side. That same year, the Tonto National Forest was created and goats were banned from the public rangeland, and all area goat ranchers were forced to switch to cattle ranching.

FLOWING SPRINGS

The East Verde River cuts a deep canyon with many deep side canyons. Each canyon bottom is thick with riparian vegetation and the hillsides are covered with brushlands and piñon and juniper woodlands. The river flows year-round and provides a couple of good swimming and wading spots to cool your heels.

This is the only area of the Rim Country to show evidence of extrusive igneous rock and widespread volcanic activity. The source of this activity, Baker Butte, sits like a thick, just-poured pancake to the north on the edge of the Rim.

Throughout time, American Indians used this area for farming until they were forced onto reservations in the latter half of the nineteenth century. They slowly drifted off the reservations and back to their gardens, but by that time much of the land had been taken over by ranchers. American Indians lost title to the land completely during the Great Depression.

The number of houses in the canyon continues to grow and the East Verde Canyon is now fairly brimming with people.

 # 14. Ash Creek Canyon

Highlights: Ash Creek Canyon, water crossings

Seasons: All year

Distance: 6.1 miles

Time: 2 hours

Difficulty Rating: Moderate

High Elevation: 4,840 feet   **Low Elevation:** 4,440 feet

USGS Topographic Maps: Payson North

Connecting Rides: 7. Doll Baby Ranch, 18. Crackerjack

Access: Travel 3 miles north on Arizona 87. Look for the dirt road on the left with a sign that says "Crackerjack Mine." There is a little room to park at the entrance to this road. You will start and end here.

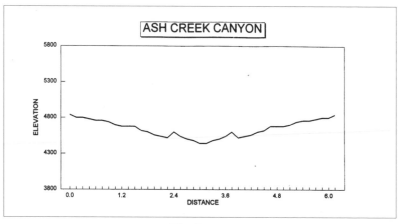

The Route

Start downhill into the wash on your right and descend as fast as you like. The log fences are here to protect the meadow (1 mile). Stay off it!

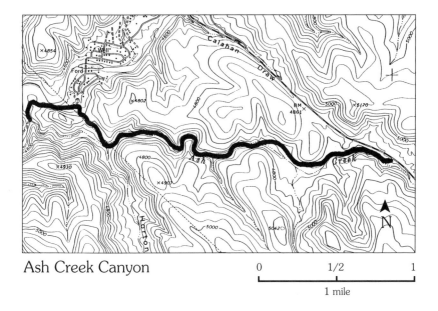

Ash Creek Canyon   0   1/2   1

1 mile

Just past the meadow the ride enters the canyon. The road crosses the creek many times through here. Be careful—there are occasionally deep potholes in the water that can send you flying. Apart from the potholes, this section is quite pleasant.

The road climbs out of the canyon and over a low hill before it drops down to a slippery concrete crossing of the East Verde River (3 miles). This is a good spot to go wading and turn around. If you are up for more riding, follow the road straight ahead to connect with the Crackerjack route (see page 94). Just remember that it is all uphill to your car from this point.

Notes

The impressive cliffs in this canyon formed from a volcanic eruption. A thick layer of ash was laid down and later buried under a sea, where it was welded together to form the rocks you see high on the canyon walls.

Crossing the creek in Ash Creek Canyon.

15. Sycamore Canyon

Highlights: Riparian vegetation

Seasons: All year

Distance: 2.3 miles

Time: 1 hour

Difficulty Rating: Very easy

High Elevation: 4,760 feet **Low Elevation:** 4,600 feet

USGS Topographic Maps: Payson North, Buckhead Mesa

Connecting Rides: 16. Flowing Springs, 18. Crackerjack

Access: Take Arizona 87 about 6 miles north to the East Verde River Canyon. The turnoff to Sycamore Canyon is on the west side of the road about 0.75 mile past the bridge. It is the second left past the bridge. Park in the little flat.

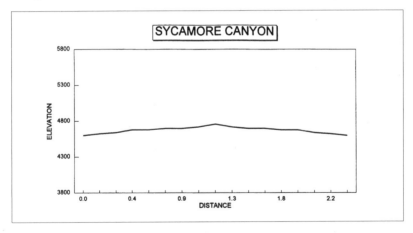

The Route

Follow the jeep trail upstream across the wash and straight ahead. It climbs a small hill before dropping back down to the wash. This

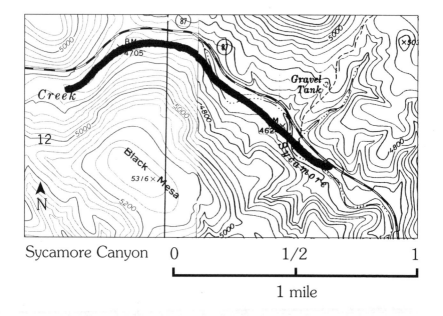

Sycamore Canyon   0   1/2   1

1 mile

route crosses the wash a couple of times. You may have to push in a couple of places, but for the most part the trail is easy to find and easy to ride. The trail dead-ends where the canyon gets deeper and more rugged.

This is a good ride for getting acclimated to the area or to test out new equipment. Though it is one of the easiest rides in the area and it follows the canyon near a highway, it is quite scenic and the canyon seems very remote.

Notes

Sycamore Canyon offers a fine example of a riparian habitat. The hills above this ride are covered with plants that grow well in dry climates. The cooler, moister canyon bottom is just right for large sycamore trees that require much more water than the surrounding plants. Even though the bottom of the canyon is mostly dry, water is always present here just below the ground's surface.

The concrete foundation at the start of this ride was part of a ranch called Asbell Place. The Holder family lived here for a while before moving to their place at Flowing Springs (see notes for Flowing Springs, page 89). In 1897 their two-month-old boy and eleven-year-old daughter, Armenta, died and were buried by the stream. Their graves are now surrounded by a white picket fence.

 # 16. Flowing Springs

Highlights: Good wading spots

Seasons: All year

Distance: 7.2 miles

Time: 2 hours

Difficulty Rating: Moderate

High Elevation: 4,900 feet   **Low Elevation:** 4,540 feet

USGS Topographic Maps: Payson South

Connecting Rides: 15. Sycamore Canyon, 18. Crackerjack

Access: Take Arizona 87 about 6 miles north to the East Verde River Canyon. The turnoff to Sycamore Canyon is on the west side of the road about 0.75 mile past the bridge. It is the second road to the left past the bridge. Park in the little flat.

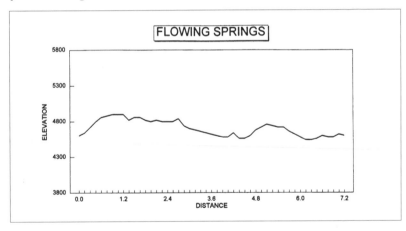

The Route

Cross Arizona 87 and head uphill to the left. There is a small wash in about 100 yards. The trail begins just beyond this wash on the right side of the highway and is immediately steep and rocky.

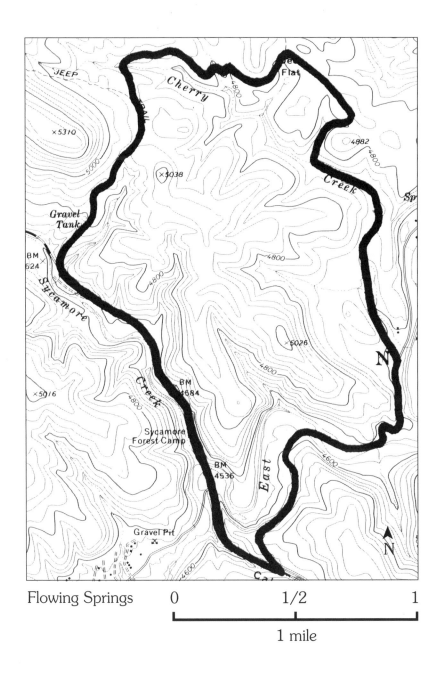

Flowing Springs

0   1/2   1

1 mile

Pass through a gate, and then under the powerlines. Look for a tank on your left (0.4 mile). At the top of this climb you will come to a wide, flat saddle. Avoid the faint road to your right and continue down the hill to your left.

This dirt section follows a barbed wire fence on your right. When you come to the intersection take the road to the right through the cattleguard gate (1.8 miles). The road drops down to the wash bottom and then ascends to a relatively flat area.

There is little undergrowth here and erosional processes are easy to see. You will come to another intersection (2.2 miles). Turn right into the cattle loading area. Pass through another gate and follow the trail along the fence line for a bit. You are looking for a trail that descends off to your right. (Avoid the wider road to your left, which leads nowhere.) If you come to another gate, you have gone too far.

The descent here is a steep, rocky single track that local ranchers use four-wheelers on to take care of their cattle. The trail quickly turns into a rocky wash where it looks like it disappears. After about 100 yards you will see the road coming out the other side.

Cross the wash a couple more times as the road levels out a bit and continues to drop down. This section is fairly smooth and you can get up some good speed if you want to. You will pass through some ranch workings and then head out to a main dirt road (4.0 miles). Turn right. This is the road through Flowing Springs.

Follow the river down to the right. There are plenty of good wading spots along here. Pass over the concrete water crossing (4.5 miles) and head up the steep hill. Once you climb out of the canyon you can see the river far below you on the right.

The road drops a bit before it turns right onto the highway (5.4 miles). Head down the steep hill to the river crossing. Just before the bridge, the entrance to the East Verde Park housing development leads off to your left. Continue over the bridge and on up the highway. Look for your car on the left.

Notes

Henry Siddles was the first settler here, arriving in 1879. He built a small cabin and did some gardening in the canyon bottom. In 1881 he sat under some trees on a nearby hill and watched Apache Indians set fire to his cabin. The homestead was later called Sidella Place.

In 1896 John and Sarah Holder, along with their eight children, moved to Sidella from New Mexico. John had served in the Confederate Army at Vicksburg, Mississippi, before moving to Texas in 1862, where he met and married Sarah. They moved to New Mexico in 1880 and came to Arizona sixteen years later. They built a stone and adobe house in the lower part of the canyon and put in a store and post office. Originally, the post office was named Holder, but was later changed to Angora in honor of the goats raised in the canyon.

There was a school at Flowing Springs after 1900.

17. Pine Canyon Overlook

Highlights: Pine Creek Canyon Gorge

Seasons: All year

Distance: 11.7 miles

Time: 4 hours

Difficulty Rating: Difficult

High Elevation: 5,320 feet   **Low Elevation:** 4,740 feet

USGS Topographic Maps: Buckhead Mesa

Connecting Rides: 18. Crackerjack

Access: Go north about 9 miles on Arizona 87. Look for a dirt jeep trail (FS 209) to the left of the highway at milepost 261. There is limited parking near the start of the road.

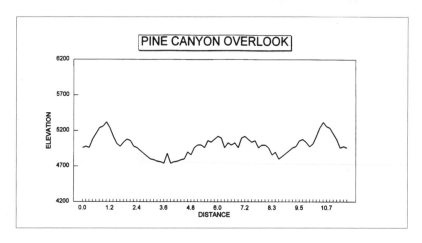

The Route

This ride begins on a narrow rutted jeep trail that quickly drops down into a small canyon (0.4 mile). This is Sycamore Creek and there is almost always water at this crossing.

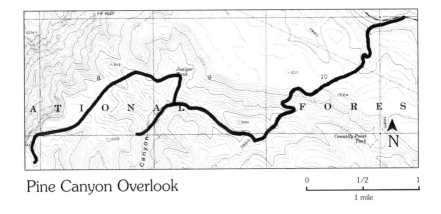

Pine Canyon Overlook

0   1/2   1

1 mile

Just after the creek the trail climbs steeply. The climb is a challenge because reefs and boulders of black volcanic rock are interspersed with loose dirt and the trail is washed out in some places. The trail levels out a bit and passes through a sloping meadow where it becomes more like a road (1 mile). You will meet a fence at the top of the hill. Pass by the gate to your right (1.2 miles) and continue straight. There are some great views of the surrounding mountains from here.

The road leads down a steep hill into Buckhead Canyon. Although the road is steep and covered with loose rocks, you have left "the volcanic nightmare" behind and should be able to open up pretty well. Just look out for the sharp left as you get near the bottom. Cross the wash bottom, then contour around a couple of small hills and washes. Watch for a jeep trail to the right that looks almost like a wash (2.1 miles). Turn right onto the trail.

The trail drops quickly into the canyon and you will ride across some rough, white limestone for a bit. Once the trail reaches the bottom of the canyon it smooths out and descends less steeply. You can really open it up through this section. This trail is seldom used and somewhat overgrown in places. Keep a sharp eye to the right to look for what seems like a giant rockfall (3.0 miles).

From here, continue down the canyon for a ways. The trail is not too rough and will cross the wash bottom a couple of times for a little technical practice. It gets progressively overgrown, then ascends suddenly out of the creek bottom. Here, the trail is almost completely

One of the many wash crossings along the Pine Canyon Overlook ride.

overgrown but you can still make it out in sections. You will climb very steeply up the west side of the canyon until you come to a small open area. Uphill and straight ahead is a small abandoned gold mine. The trail to the right contours around until it ends at a wash. Turn around here (3.7 miles) and head back toward the rockfall, where you will turn left (4.5 miles).

The jeep trail up the rockfall is very steep and probably unrideable, but give it a try. Climb up to the top of the hill and then begin your descent. Look in the canyon bottom to your left for Juniper Tank. The trail makes a couple of switchbacks before dumping you into the rocky wash bottom. Turn up the wash until you come to the small dam holding Juniper Tank (4.8 miles).

Look for the trail going off to the left, or west, of Juniper Tank. Once you find it, the trail will be easy to follow. It climbs over a couple of low ridges and makes some short descents. The farther you get along the trail the better the views become. Make a steep descent to a saddle and stop here for a fantastic view (6.3 miles).

The canyon to your right is Pine Creek Canyon. Although you cannot see it from here, the Tonto Natural Bridge is about 1 mile

Flowing Springs

upstream. Directly across the canyon is the boundary for the Mazatzal Wilderness Area. If it is not too windy, you should be able to hear the sound of water rushing over the rocks about 800 feet below.

Continue up the hill from the saddle. The ridge gets narrower and narrower, and the views from all sides get better and better. Ride to the highest point of the hill. You will see that the road continues down off the ridge toward the south but peters out at a dead-end. This is a good spot to turn around (6.6 miles).

Follow the same route back, remembering to turn left after coming down the rockfall (8.6 miles) and at the main dirt road.

Notes

This is the only ride in this book that takes you over extrusive igneous rock in the form of an old lava flow.

 **18. Crackerjack**

Highlights: Spectacular views, Crackerjack Mine, East Verde River

Seasons: All year

Distance: 14.6 miles

Time: 5 hours

Difficulty Rating: Difficult

High Elevation: 5,320 feet   **Low Elevation:** 4,380 feet

USGS Topographic Maps: Buckhead Mesa, Payson North

Connecting Rides: 7. Doll Baby Ranch, 14. Ash Creek Canyon, 15. Sycamore Canyon, 16. Flowing Springs, 17. Pine Canyon Overlook

Access: Go north about 9 miles on Arizona 87. Look for a dirt jeep trail (FS 209) to the left of the highway at milepost 261. There is limited parking near the start of the road.

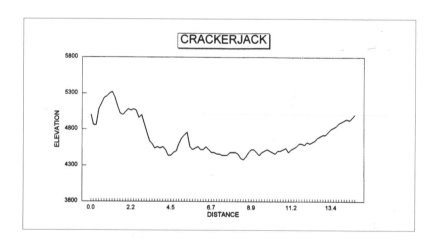

The Route

This ride begins on a narrow rutted jeep trail that quickly drops down into a small canyon (0.4 mile).

Just after the creek the trail climbs steeply. The trail is washed out in some places and the rocks make the climb challenging. The trail levels out a bit and passes through a sloping meadow area where it becomes more like a road (1.0 mile). Continue straight when you get to the top of the hill, passing by a fence and a gate to your right (1.2 miles).

The road leads down a steep hill into Buckhead Canyon. Cross the wash bottom, then contour around a couple of small hills and washes (2.1 miles). Keep following the main road. Head over the small saddle into a canyon. Stay to the left if you are in doubt, as this ride drops in and contours out of canyons. At the one faint intersection you meet, make sure you turn to the left, staying on FS 209 (3.6 miles).

The views from here are fantastic. Climb up a steep hill to get to the Crackerjack Mine Road, which is marked (5.4 miles). Turn left. The steep climbing continues until you reach the top of the hill.

To your right is a pile of mine tailings and two deep mine shafts. Do not get too close to these shafts as they may cave in without warning. There are several jeep trails in this area. Be sure to stick to the main road.

You may have to walk your bike down this very steep, rocky hill until you get to what is left of Crackerjack Mine. The road smooths out past the mine and winds around the side of the hill. It suddenly drops into Brushy Canyon, which is full of sycamore and cottonwood trees.

The road climbs over a saddle where the river makes a large bend to the south, then drops back down to a concrete crossing of the East Verde River (9.4 miles). This is an excellent wading pool.

As you come out of the river bottom you can see the houses at East Verde Park. Take the road to your left, blocked to cars by a large gate, that leads into the development (9.8 miles).

Head down the steep hill, straight ahead, through the housing development and cross the river again (10.3 miles). Ride east through the rest of East Verde Estates.

As you leave the subdivision, but before you get to the highway, there are several excellent swimming and wading holes. Turn left onto

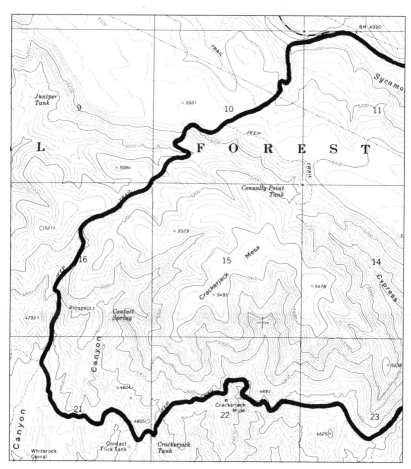

Crackerjack

Arizona 87 (11.2 miles) and follow it uphill all the way back to your car. (Sorry about the paved miles!)

Notes

The first Apache Indians to move to the Rim Country arrived in the mid-1500s. They are known as the Tonto Apaches and were less

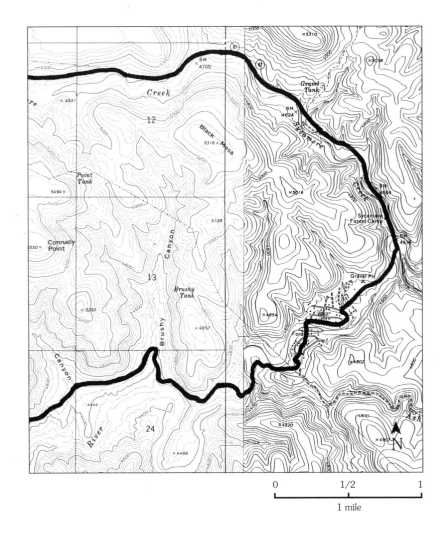

0   1/2   1

1 mile

nomadic and more peaceful than their famous cousins to the south-east. In the 1870s the Tonto Apaches succumbed to the Springfield Rifle and the Colt Pistol. The Tontos were relocated to the Fort Verde reservation and later moved to San Carlos in 1875. They did not like San Carlos, so they walked back to the Payson area in 1886 after the guards were removed from the reservation.

They moved into the East Verde Park and began to farm. The land was officially homesteaded by Delia Chapman, and the little farm came to be called Indian Delia's Place. During the Great Depression the tribe sold this spot for $500 to pay its federal tax bill. The Tonto Apaches now live on a small reservation just south of Payson.

In 1883 Samuel and Mary Ann Conley brought two children and thirty-five horses with them from Oregon to East Verde Park. The wagon trip took three months. They were slowed by the birth of several colts along the way. The horses were difficult to handle because the children had thrown the hobbles out of the wagon when no one was looking. They built a home from wood they bought in Payson. They raised cattle in the area and built some corrals high on the hills, hence the name Conley Points.

UNDER THE DIAMOND RIM

This is the land of prehistoric Native Americans. Big game hunters subsisted on dwindling herds of mammoth or bison as early as twelve thousand years ago. The people lived in small bands and built pit-houses. By 1000 A.D. some of these sites had developed into small, pueblo-style villages. These villages grew until they were mysteriously abandoned sometime after 1200 A.D. The site of one of the largest of these villages is located at Shoofly Ruins on the Houston Mesa.

The area is a mix of granite hills and limestone flats, dominated by the Diamond Rim to the northeast. The East Verde River is to the northwest, and the edge of the Houston Mesa is to the south.

The vegetation is a mix of piñon and juniper woodlands, brush-lands, and grasslands.

19. Edge of Mesa Del

Highlights: Excellent view of Payson

Seasons: All year

Distance: 3.4 miles

Time: 1 hour

Difficulty Rating: Easy

High Elevation: 5,350 feet   **Low Elevation:** 5,240 feet

USGS Topographic Maps: Payson North

Access: Head 2 miles north on Arizona 87. Turn right on Houston Mesa Road. Drive up to the edge of the mesa and park near the fence on the right.

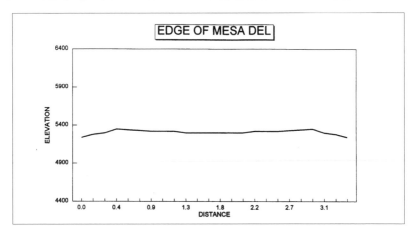

The Route

Cross over the pavement and look for the rough road leading up the hill just to the north of the fence line. It climbs right to the edge of the rim. You can follow along the edge and enjoy some great views.

Under the Diamond Rim

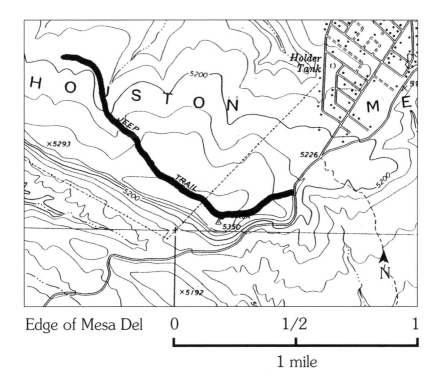

Edge of Mesa Del   0   1/2   1

1 mile

Look for an old, dead-end logging road leading off to your right. Turn around anywhere you want.

Notes

The edge of Houston Mesa extends east about 7 miles all the way to Diamond Point. This mesa was named after Sam Houston (see Pocket Cabin Trail, page 189). Sam was killed when the stirrup to his saddle caught on his pistol scabbard and discharged the weapon, hitting him in the leg. He bled to death before he could get any help.

The view from the edge of Houston Mesa.

Under the Diamond Rim

 # 20. Walnut Flats

Highlights: Shoofly Indian Ruins

Seasons: All year

Distance: 4 miles, or 9 miles if you take all the options

Time: 1.5 to 4 hours

Difficulty Rating: Easy

High Elevation: 5,300 feet   **Low Elevation:** 5,100 feet

USGS Topographic Maps: Payson North, Diamond Point

Connecting Rides: 21. Shoofly and the River, 24. The Crossings

Access: Travel north on Arizona 87 about 2 miles and turn east on Houston Mesa Road. Follow the paved road over the edge of the mesa and bear right at the entrance to the Mesa del Caballo housing development. The parking area for the Shoofly Ruins is on your right about 1 mile past the General Store.

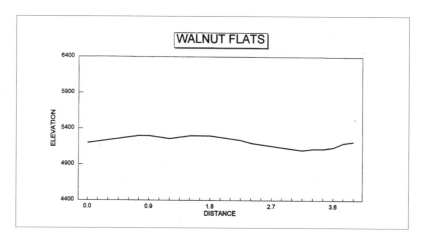

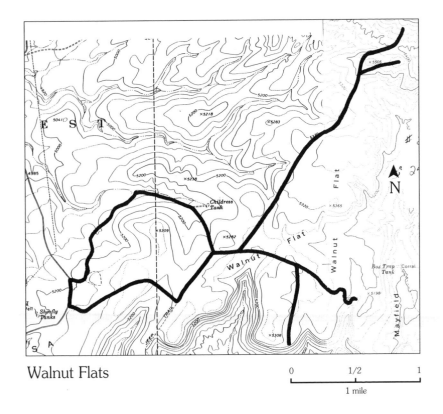

Walnut Flats

0   1/2   1

1 mile

The Route

Head out of the Shoofly parking lot and turn left on Houston Mesa Road. Go uphill on the paved road until you come to a cattle loading chute on your right (0.3 mile). The dirt track you want to take is to the left, directly opposite of the loading chute.

This track is deeply rutted with some rocky sections, but it is generally flat until you come to a small hill. Ride down this rocky section and turn left when you get to the first intersection (1.3 miles). Continue over the flats until you reach the next intersection (1.9 miles). If you want to explore some of the extensions described just after this route description, they begin at this intersection.

If not, stay to the left to follow the main route. The road immediately plummets down rugged limestone. This descent is very rocky so you should be careful here. At the bottom of the hill you will come to Childress Tank (2.5 miles), which is full of muddy water year-round. The road back to the ruins leads away from the tank to your left. It follows along the valley bottom for a while, then rises out of it to the left. The road divides a number of times in this section, as people have tried to avoid mud holes. All of the splits lead back to the same route, except for *one* that you have to be careful about: As you begin to climb the hill there is a road leading off to the right (3.6 miles). It looks like another way around one of those mud holes, but this road never rejoins the main one. The road you want is the steep, rocky one to the left.

Just after the steep hill you meet a gate that opens into the ruins area. The picnic ramadas were built a couple of years ago by boy scouts doing their Eagle project.

The ruins are undeveloped, unlike others you may have visited in Arizona, but they are just as interesting. Please be courteous while in the ruins and do not ride your bike near them.

Route Extensions

Starting at the second intersection along the route, turn to your right and then take the first left. Cruise along this mostly flat area for about 2 miles until you get to a steep, rocky, unrideable hill. Push up this hill. At the top you will find another intersection.

The road to the left runs down the north side of the hill and then crosses a wash. After you pass through a gate the road peters out on the open hillside straight ahead. There used to be a jeep trail to the top of the Diamond Rim from here, but a number of years ago the Forest Service put a fence line right down the middle of this trail and let the undergrowth grow back. It is impossible to follow now. But the open hillside is a good spot for riding around. Follow the road back to the intersection.

If you take the road to the south, it slowly ascends to the top of a small hill and then dies out. The trail is indefinite but you can ride about anywhere; just don't lose the trail back. This is another good spot for riding around. Return to the intersection.

At the first intersection along the route (just before the steep rocky descent into Childress Tank) you can take the road to the south. Follow this trail up over the small hill and take your first right. Follow this jeep trail straight out to the edge of the mesa. There are good views of the Star Valley below you, Diamond Point (with its radio and lookout towers) to your left, and the impressive cliffs above Stewart Pocket straight ahead. Turn around and return to the road you were on. If you turn right, the road snakes gently downward and ends in a thick grove of trees near the edge of the mesa after about a mile. The views are not so good here as at the last lookout. Turn around and return by the same route.

These extensions may be confusing. Just remember to always return the way you came. This area is called Walnut Flats and is a great area just to cruise.

Remains of a stone room excavated at the Shoofly Ruins.

Under the Diamond Rim

Notes

Shoofly village was built between 1000 and 1250 A.D. by people closely related to the Hohokam and Salado peoples to the south. The people who lived here, however, developed their own culture. The village contains eighty-seven rooms and many courtyards, all surrounded by a wall. The entire village occupies about four acres. The earliest buildings were oval and the later buildings were rectangular and clustered close to the center of the site. The courtyards, archaeologists believe, suggest that people had their own families or social identities within the larger group.

There are springs nearby, so the town was well supplied with water. Corn and a number of grinding stones have been found here, suggesting that agriculture was important. About forty sites have been located within 3 miles of the village, many near check dams and farming terraces. Archaeologists feel that the people of the village may have used the outlying sites during the farming season.

A more thorough description of the history of the prehistoric inhabitants of this area is at the front of this book.

21. Shoofly and the River

Highlights: Shoofly Ruins, East Verde River

Seasons: All year

Distance: 9.5 miles

Time: 3 hours

Difficulty Rating: Difficult

High Elevation: 5,240 feet   **Low Elevation:** 4,840 feet

USGS Topographic Maps: Payson North

Access: Travel north on Arizona 87 about 2 miles and turn east on Houston Mesa Road. Follow the paved road over the edge of the mesa and bear right at the entrance to the Mesa del Caballo housing development. The parking area for the Shoofly Ruins is on your right about 1 mile past the General Store.

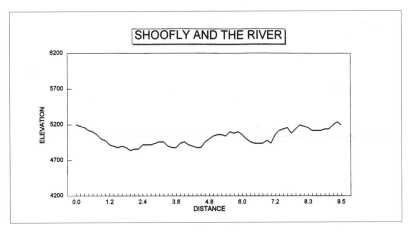

The Route

Go back out onto Houston Mesa Road and turn right. It is paved for the first bit, but there will be plenty of dirt trails for you to work on

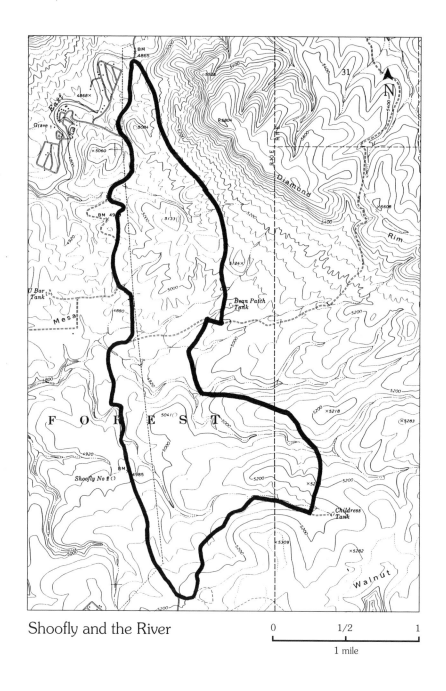

Shoofly and the River

later. Bomb down this hill for 4.2 miles. The road is well maintained but full of washboards. Although the road is mostly downhill, there are enough ascents to remind you that you are in the mountains.

As you ride down into the East Verde River Canyon the cliffs of the Diamond Rim rise up impressively before you. There is one turn you need to take on this very quick descent, at a signed Y in the road. You will need to go to the left. The road to the right is FS 198.

Once you get to the river the road is paved again for a short distance on either side of the new bridge. Just past the "Ice Forms on Bridge First" sign look for a trail leading into the woods on your right. This was once a popular four-wheeling area, but the Forest Service has since blocked it off with piles of dirt, so you may have to look a bit for the trail.

Head to the east on the trail. After just a few yards, look for another jeep trail leading off to your right. If you come to an area that has been torn up to discourage four-wheeling, you have gone too far.

For the next mile the trend of the trail is generally uphill. However, since the trail is traversing the front of the hill, there are a number of washes to cross. You will encounter a number of short, steep descents, followed by longer, but equally steep climbs. You may have to push your bike at times. Be careful through here as the trail is made of loosely packed, coarse granite gravel and can be very slippery (it is like riding over a pile of ball bearings).

After you top out on the hill you can see the houses and water tanks of the Mesa del Caballo subdivision ahead of you. The distant mountain peeking over the top of the houses is Mount Ord. From this hill, blast down the well-defined road until you get to a tangle of roads.

Take the left turn at each of the first two intersections and then take the next right. If you get to Bean Patch Tank, an obvious party hole, take the nearest road off to your right. After a few yards all of these roads will dump you onto FS 198.

Turn right on FS 198 and go down into the small wash. Look for the drainage pipe under the road, and the trail leading off to your left. If you have had enough you can bail out here. Simply follow FS 198 back to Houston Mesa Road, turn left, and ride back to Shoofly. (Returning via Houston Mesa Road doesn't save much mileage, but from here on the trail is very rough, and sometimes difficult to follow. Some may prefer the road.)

If you take the trail, follow it off to your left across a couple of small washes. Pass a small barbed wire corral on your left.

As you ride through here you will notice a change in the rocks. Up to this point you have been riding through an area of granite with its coarsely packed sand and round, smooth rocks. You are now passing through an area of limestone. The rocks here are much more jagged and broken. There is no sand and the trail passes over continuous fields of broken rock. It is a challenge to stay on the bike as you get bounced around. Be sure and watch for the large, sharp rocks. They can shred your sidewalls.

Cross over the top of the small hill and ride down into the next wash. This wash is steep-sided, and very rocky. Look across the wash and you will see the trail leading up the opposite hill. As you go up the hill the trail tends to swing off to the left.

During this climb the trail seems to disappear, but as you move on you will see where the road keeps going. (That darned limestone just doesn't hold too many tire tracks!) Every once in a while you will see where trucks have taken this route some time before.

The trail eventually tops out on this hill and drops you into another steep-sided wash. When you climb out the other side you will see a small path going up the wash to your left, and another small path leading down the wash to your right. Do not take either one of these trails. The trail you want goes straight ahead, up the next hill.

Pedal up this steep hill and pass through a range gate on your way down into the Childress Tank area. Once you get into the flat wash bottom you will notice that the limestone has (thankfully!) given way to dirt. Childress Tank is close by to your left and typically has water in it year-round.

Take the road off to your right. It splits and comes back together several times, but all of the splits lead back to the main route. This area can be very muddy in the spring and after a rainfall.

After several hundred yards the road climbs more steeply to your left. Just after the road gets even more steep, there is a road you will want to take off to the right. Take the rocky climb to the left instead. At the top of the ridge pass through the gate into Shoofly Ruins Park. Please respect the other visitors by not riding your bike around the ruins. A dirt road outside of the fence leads around the perimeter of the ruins, if you are into a little more exploring.

 # 22. Over the Diamond Rim

Highlights: Views from Diamond Rim, Pyeatt Draw

Seasons: All year, except after a snowstorm

Distance: 10.7 miles

Time: 3 hours

Difficulty Rating: Difficult

High Elevation: 5,840 feet   **Low Elevation:** 4,900 feet

USGS Topographic Maps: Payson North and Diamond Point

Connecting Rides: 35. Pyeatt Draw

Access: Travel north on Arizona 87 about 2 miles and turn east on Houston Mesa Road. Follow the paved road over the edge of the mesa and bear right at the entrance to the Mesa del Caballo housing development, past the Shoofly Ruins and onto the dirt road. Follow the road until you come to a signed intersection for FS 198, about 8 miles from the turn onto Houston Mesa Road.

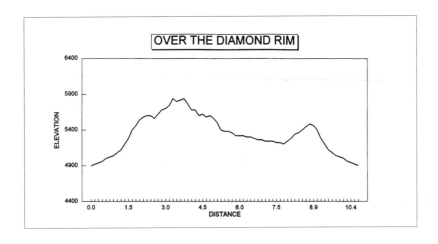

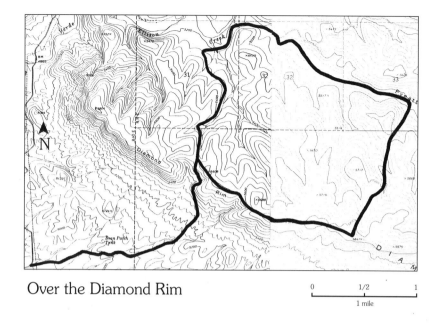

Over the Diamond Rim

0	1/2	1

1 mile

The Route

Start on FS 198 as it climbs gently to the east. The road is very easy to follow. The Forest Service scrapes it and there are drainage pipes, so it stays in pretty good shape.

You will climb for a while before going down a very short hill into a wash. The climb begins in earnest here. The road is steep as it goes up the face of Diamond Rim and there are some spots that are very tough to ride.

At the top of the hill (1.9 miles) cross a cattleguard and take the jeep trail to the right, immediately past the fence line. The route gets steeper here as you climb up on top of the Diamond Rim. The views from here are spectacular and you can see for many miles to the west. The Mogollon Rim rises to your right and in the near distance you can see where the East Verde River emerges from behind the Diamond Rim.

Continue along the trail. At the top of one of the hills you will come to a T-intersection. Take a moment to stop here. There used to be a trail that went off the rim, and the start of it is on your right. The Forest Service built a fence line down the center of this road and it is impossible to take it now because of dense brush growth.

Go to the left and hang on—the first part of this hill is a "white-knuckler." As soon as you leave the rim you will notice that the trees change from piñon and juniper to ponderosa pine. The air will be noticeably cooler and moister.

After a few hundred yards the trail levels out and you will be able to let go of the brakes a bit. Cross over three small rises, each one just after a small wash. After the third hill, the trail drops down into a wide wash with large shelves of rock. This is Pyeatt Draw (5.2 miles).

Turn left on the dirt road just this side of the wash. This road gently spills down the wash. If you want to put it in high gear and hammer, you can really go. However, this area is so beautiful you will want to take it slow.

The road crosses the wash a couple of times and you might have to walk your bike in places. After what seems like just a couple of minutes, you will come to the end of the Pyeatt Draw Trail when it T's into FS 198 (7.0 miles).

FS 198 is maintained and easy to follow. Take it to the left and up the hill. The climb is not too steep until you get to the crest of the hill, and then it gets quite steep. Finally, you arrive at the cattleguard (8.8 miles).

Take the road straight down the front of Diamond Rim and back to your car. The descent is another white-knuckler, but it eventually levels out and allows you to fly over the last mile.

Notes

Pyeatt Draw, as well as all the other washes in this area, was changed during the floods of the 1992–93 winter. These floods were some of the worst in many years and nearly all of the creeks and washes in this area were widened, scoured, and changed. Once lush with grasses, the area's floodplain is now strewn with rocks and boulders; what were once small washes in the middle of meadows are now wide rock fields.

23. Gilliland Gap

Highlights: Diamond Rim views, single track

Seasons: All year, except after a snowstorm

Distance: 17.0 miles

Time: 6 hours

Difficulty Rating: Strenuous

High Elevation: 5,920 feet   **Low Elevation:** 4,780 feet

USGS Topographic Maps: Payson North, Diamond Point

Connecting Rides: 35. Pyeatt Draw, 45. Mayor's Cup, 46. Schoolhouse Canyon

Access: Head 4 miles east on Arizona 260, passing through Star Valley. Look for a dirt road leading to the north from the highway at the east end of Star Valley. It is past the car dealership and just before the highway narrows. Turn left onto the dirt road (FS 433) and follow it for about 0.75 mile until it dead-ends at a gravel pit. Park here.

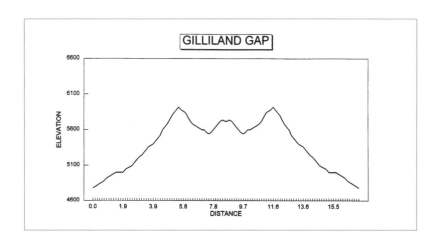

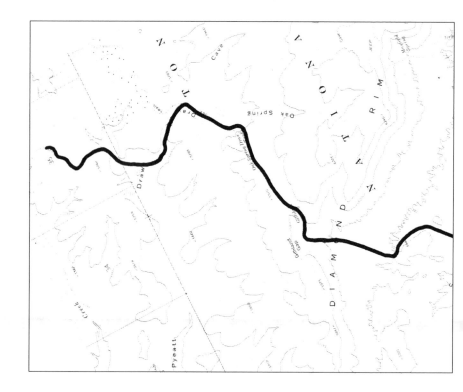

The Route

The trail starts to the north of the gravel pit on the other side of the wash. It is easy to see as this is a favorite spot for the local motorized off-road set. Follow the trail to the east as it climbs up the wash. Ignore the trails to the left.

After a while the trail climbs away from the wash bottom and tops out at a short, steep hill. From here the trail rolls a bit, trending downhill. Just after this "flat" section, a road leads off to the right (1.5 miles). This is the route to Schoolhouse Canyon. You will want to continue straight ahead.

Cross a couple more washes until you come to a four-way intersection in a wash bottom (2.1 miles). The trail to the right dead-ends up the wash a ways at a couple of cattle feeding stations. The trail to the left dead-ends at an old corral and stock tank after about 100 yards. The trail you want to take goes straight ahead over the little hill.

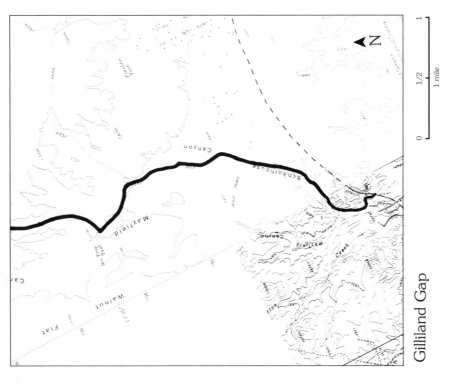

Just after the hill the trail passes into another wash and bends to the east again. The trail is extremely sandy so you may have to push. After a while, the wash narrows and is less sandy. It climbs steadily the closer you get to the mountains. Notice that the higher you go, the thicker and larger the riparian vegetation becomes.

The trail tops out of the canyon to the left and comes to an intersection by a cow feeding shed (4.0 miles). Turn right. Pass through a thick stand of manzanita as you work your way up the steep hill.

Drop briefly into Mayfield Canyon. There is permanent water in this area and the many pools attract bugs and wildlife. The trail stays to the right of the pools, sometimes high above them.

As you get into the Gilliland Gap a fence blocks your path (4.8 miles). This fence is here to control access to Gilliland Springs. Skirt around the fence to your right. The trail climbs a steep hill just after you pass the springs. It is rocky here and may be difficult to follow.

Cross a rough wash and continue on the obscure trail. Pass a small tank around to the right. It is a little farther to Oak Spring Draw

Tank (6.1 miles). The trail is hard to the right just after the tank. There is another good-looking trail to the left, but it dead-ends in a pine thicket not too far from here. Pass through a range gate and cross over the draw.

The trail drops down to an intersection just after a rocky section of the wash (6.7 miles). The trail to the right leads over a small hill and into the Diamond Point summer homes. Take the trail to the left across the wash and through another range gate (7.0 miles). The road descends smoothly from here.

Pyeatt Draw is easy to spot, as it is filled with huge slabs of rock (7.5 miles). Quickly cross the wash two more times and come to an intersection (7.8 miles). Ignore the good road to the right that leads back into the summer home area. Follow the trail up the hill by the stock tank, turning to the right. The road to the left just after the tank leads out a ridge line to a former logging spot. This spur is about 1 mile long and is nice for exploring.

The trail to the right goes down a small hill and ends on FS 198. Turn around here and follow the same route back.

Notes

Gilliland Gap is named after John Gilliland, who arrived in Arizona from Texas in 1879. He was foreman for the Stinson Ranch and was shot during the Pleasant Valley War by John and Jim Tewksbury, supposedly while they were cleaning a rifle. Gilliland survived the shooting and the Tewksburys had to stand trial for the incident, although I haven't been able to find out what the verdict was.

The Gap was a good area to move cattle down to from the higher country to the north of here because of the permanent water found along the way.

WHISPERING PINES

This area is squeezed between the Diamond Rim and the Mogollon Rim on the upper reaches of the East Verde River. The presence of so many tall mountains gives Whispering Pines a true alpine feel. The abundance of water creates thick ponderosa pine forests and vibrant patches of wild berries.

Originally homesteaded in 1874 by an Italian miner named Bartholomeo Belluzzi, Whispering Pines has been subdivided and sold and now contains a number of summer homes.

The forest floor is composed mainly of pine needles, twigs, and leaves lying over a granite base. The washes are filled with granite as well as bits of sedimentary rock washed down from the edge of the Rim.

The area is webbed with old logging roads. Most of these are great for exploring, but they tend to dead-end high up on the side of the Rim.

The terminus of the trans-rim pipeline is located at a pump house along the river at the Washington Park Trailhead. This pipeline transports water from the Blue Ridge Reservoir to the Verde River drainage basin. Built in 1965 by the Phelps Dodge Corporation, the pump house is used to pay the Salt River Project back for water used in mining at Morenci.

24. The Crossings

Highlights: East Verde River

Seasons: All year

Distance: 13.8 miles

Time: 4 hours

Difficulty Rating: Moderate

High Elevation: 5,240 feet   **Low Elevation:** 4,840 feet

USGS Topographic Maps: Payson North, Kehl Ridge

Connecting Rides: 20. Walnut Flats, 21. Shoofly and the River, 22. Over the Diamond Rim, 25. Control Road West, 26. Washington Park, 27. Whispering Pines

Access: Travel north on Arizona 87 about 2 miles and turn east on Houston Mesa Road. Follow the paved road over the edge of the mesa and bear right at the entrance to the Mesa del Caballo housing development. Park at the parking area for the Shoofly Ruins, on your right about 1 mile past the General Store.

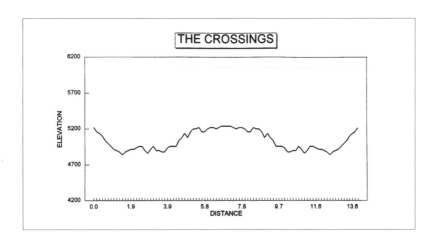

The Route

Turn right and head down the paved road. This road will soon turn to dirt. This section is heavily washboarded because of the amount of vehicle traffic. Cross the wash and go left at the Y-intersection (1.6 miles). To your left is Sunflower Mesa and the Wonder Valley/Freedom Acres subdivision.

Climb over the next hill and you will be at the first crossing (3.7 miles). After the first crossing you will climb over another small hill and come close to the river at the semideveloped Water Wheel camping spot.

The road climbs steeply here, passing near a popular—but dangerous—cliff to the right (4.7miles). The road drops down to the river and crosses it again. After the river crossing look for a road on your right (5.2 miles). This leads to the parking lot for Cold Springs.

If you want to go to the springs and the small waterfall, take your bike down the steep trail past the gate. At the bottom of the hill follow the path up to the springs. This is a very popular swimming hole so you shouldn't have any trouble finding it.

When you get back to the main road continue to follow it up the river, crossing it once more before you get to the paved road that travels through the Whispering Pines subdivision. On the other side of the subdivision look for the steel bridge over the river. Turn around here.

Notes

Before the winter of 1992–93 there was a concrete water crossing below the new bridge at the first crossing. The river flooded several times that winter and completely altered the crossing, forcing the county to build this bridge. This crossing was the only one of the three low water crossings that was affected by the flood because of the high volume of water here. Ellison Creek, which drains a large area to the east of here (see The Hidden Forests section), dumps into the East Verde River just above this spot. The forests in the Ellison Creek drainage were damaged extensively by the 1990 Dude Fire and could not hold the water that was being dumped by all the rains of the 1992–93 winter. Ellison Creek flooded severely and added to the flooding of the East Verde River. The roaring water just ripped out the crossing.

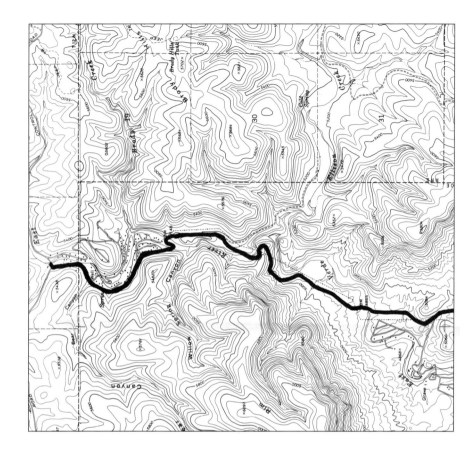

There are ruins of an old water-driven mill at the Water Wheel campsite.

Many people have died on the cliffs near the second water crossing because the cliffs are so easy to get to. You don't have to climb them to get on top; just park your bike and walk over to the edge. If you are going to stop at these cliffs, please be careful.

For information about the subdivision, *see* Washington Park (page 129).

Whispering Pines

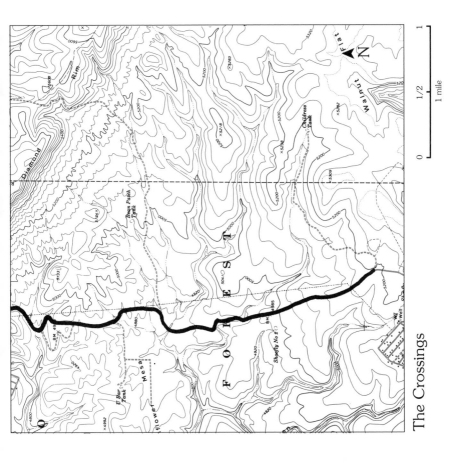

The Crossings

The old water wheel still stands at Water Wheel campsite.

 # 25. Control Road West

Highlights: Hilly ride through the forest

Seasons: All year, except after a snowstorm

Distance: 18.4 miles

Time: 4 hours

Difficulty Rating: Moderate, but long

High Elevation: 5,680 feet   **Low Elevation:** 5,180 feet

USGS Topographic Maps: Kehl Ridge, Payson North, Buckhead Mesa

Connecting Rides: 24. The Crossings, 26. Washington Park, 27. Whispering Pines

Access: Follow Arizona 87 north 2 miles out of Payson to Houston Mesa Road. Turn right and follow the road over the Rim, past the Mesa del Caballo subdivision and the Shoofly Ruins. The road crosses the East Verde River three times and passes through the Whispering Pines subdivision before reaching the steel bridge, about 8 miles past the General Store. (If you are after a strenuous ride, you can start this ride at the Shoofly Ruins.) Start and end at the parking area about 0.3 mile east of the bridge along the left side of the road.

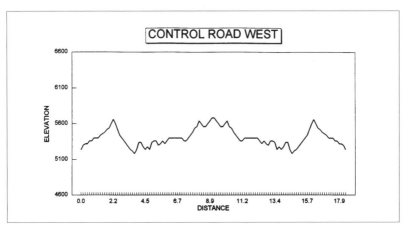

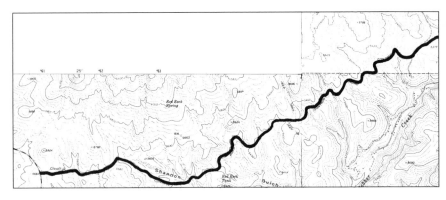

Control Road West

The Route

Cross back over the bridge and head straight on FS 64 at the intersection with Houston Mesa Road. In fact, you will always go straight on this ride. Climb up steadily away from the river and cross over the top of the ridge. Descend into Webber Creek (it is steep at first). At the creek (3.9 miles) is an intersection with Camp Geronimo to your right and Geronimo Estates subdivision down the road to your left. Continue straight on FS 64.

Climb up out of Webber Creek. The road climbs up to chaparral-covered ridges and drops down into woods and creeks again and again until it reaches Highway 87 (9.3 miles). Turn around here.

Notes

Webber Creek was so named on a map made by Colonel Nevin Webber after he led a scouting party through here in 1868.

If you have the time, head up to Camp Geronimo. If you are a man who was raised in Arizona, you probably went to this boy scout camp at least once while you were growing up. The development at the camp is extensive, although the boy scouts take good care of the

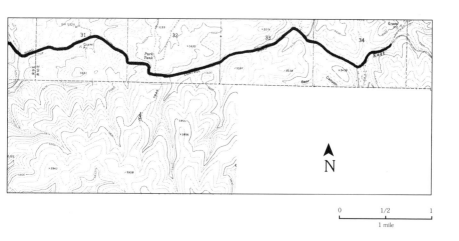

Steel bridge at the start of the Control Road West ride.

place. Be sure to ask for permission to ride in the camp before you enter, especially if there are campers there.

The big mesa sticking out from the Rim ahead of you on the first leg of this ride is Milk Ranch Point. A Mormon family ran a dairy farm here during construction of the railroad through Winslow. The family sold milk to the workers.

26. Washington Park

Highlights: Upper East Verde River, railroad tunnel

Seasons: Spring through fall

Distance: 12.5 miles

Time: 4 hours

Difficulty Rating: Difficult

High Elevation: 6,560 feet (tunnel)   **Low Elevation:** 5,240 feet

USGS Topographic Maps: Kehl Ridge, Dane Canyon

Connecting Rides: 24. The Crossings, 25. Control Road West,
27. Whispering Pines

Access: Follow Arizona 87 2.0 miles north out of Payson to Houston
Mesa Road. Turn right and follow the road over the Rim past the
Mesa del Caballo subdivision and the Shoofly Ruins. The road crosses
the East Verde River three times and passes through the Whispering
Pines subdivision before reaching the steel bridge, about 8.0 miles
past the General Store. (If you are after a strenuous ride, you can start
this ride at the Shoofly Ruins. Start and end at the parking area about
0.3 mile east of the bridge along the left side of the road.)

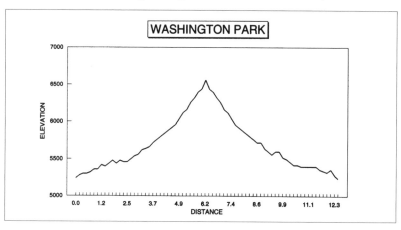

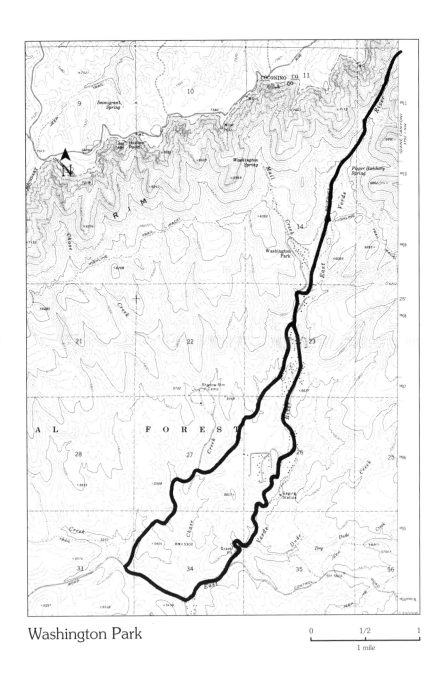

Washington Park

```
0          1/2          1
       1 mile
```

Whispering Pines

The Route

Follow the sign for FS 199 and cross the East Verde River. Dude Creek comes into the river just upstream from this spot. Follow the main road uphill past the quarry and turn left at the first intersection (0.8 mile). Follow the main road into the summer home area, past several closed gates. This is private land.

Cross the river (1.5 miles) and you are back into national forest land. The road becomes much rougher. This is a popular camping spot and you will see plenty of evidence of overuse. After several hundred yards the road passes again onto private land in the Washington Park subdivision, just after a small waterfall. The road is much better here. Continue straight until you pass the river once again and come to FS 32, a main dirt road (2.7 miles). Turn right and continue uphill.

Turn right again at the sign for the pump station (3.1 miles). The road is marked with a sign for the Washington Park Trailhead. Be sure to visit the pump station while you are here. Continue up the canyon to the trailhead. Take hiking trail 290 west of the parking area and corral.

The trail follows the pipeline. There is a lot of water here, both from springs and from many leaks in the pipe. The trail becomes increasingly steep and rocky, but the vegetation is lush and the air is cool. Some pitches may be too steep to ride. Look to your right where the canyon widens out a bit for the sign marking the trail to the railroad tunnel. You won't be able to ride all the way to the tunnel, but go ahead and walk the 0.25 mile up to look at it. Turn around here (5.6 miles).

If you are feeling adventurous, you can get to the top of the Rim from the tunnel trail junction. The old wagon road is on the east side of the canyon. It is very steep and difficult to find, but well worth the effort as you will see some of the rock fills put in over 100 years ago. These fills were put here to help the wagons get through. Imagine *that* as you push! At the top is a historical marker for the Battle of Big Dry Wash and General Springs Cabin, just down the draw straight ahead.

Follow the trail back the way you came all the way past the pump station (8.1 miles). But rather than turning into the Washington Park subdivision, stick to the right and bomb down the wide, dirt freeway. This road T's at Control Road (FS 64, 11.4 miles). Turn left and take this road back over the bridge to your car.

Notes

Dude Creek is named after Frank McClintock, who lived upstream from the confluence of the creek and the East Verde River. He was from the city, so people referred to him as a "city dude." The Dude Fire got its name from the fact that it started near the creek.

Whispering Pines was first settled in 1874 by John Beluzzi. He was born in Genoa, Italy, in 1848 and longed to sail. In 1867 he got a job aboard an Italian ship and was ready to see the world. He developed circulatory problems in his legs and jumped ship in San Francisco to avoid having them amputated. He learned about mining and worked his way inland from San Francisco, eventually winding up in Globe, Arizona. He and his friend, Louis Barnini (who had traveled on that same Italian ship), heard about homesteading opportunities in Payson and decided to give it a shot. They picked out the place on a map and then traveled there, setting up the ranch they called the Rim Trail Ranch. Rimrock School was opened in 1900. The area is now known as Whispering Pines.

The railroad tunnel was built between 1885 and 1887. The Arizona Mineral Belt Railroad Company wanted to lay tracks from Globe to meet the transcontinental railroad in Flagstaff. The hardest part of the line would be getting the trains over the Rim. The tunnel was planned so that the trains could maintain a steady incline. It was to cut underneath the edge of the Rim and open out into a canyon on the north side. Believers in the project were asked to bring their own mules to the site. The railroad provided the tools and the miners were paid in stocks. Everyone thought they would get rich if they could get the valuable minerals out of Globe to the national markets by rail, then an inexpensive means of transport. The miners toiled away at the tunnel, digging out the first 75 feet, before the railroad surveyor thought he found a better route and abandoned the project. The railroad was never completed, and the investors lost all of their money when the county sheriff sold the line to a Flagstaff lumber company. As late as the 1920s, piles of ties lay along the proposed right-of-way south of Mormon Lake.

Elwood Pyle ran a burro pack train between Payson and Flagstaff from 1892 to the early 1900s. In the summer he would lead his burros over the Rim from Washington Park to Flagstaff. Elwood and his wife Sarah were originally from Kansas, where they farmed and sold windmills. From there, Elwood took his business to Los Angeles, where Sarah developed asthma. They exchanged their property sight-unseen for a place in Star Valley in 1890. In 1893 they moved to Bonita Creek, a couple of miles east of Washington Park, where they started an orchard and a large garden.

At the top of the Rim is General Springs Cabin. Gen. George Crook found the springs here in 1871 while hiding from a band of Apache Indians. The springs came to be known as General Springs and the cabin was built here later.

There are conflicting accounts of what happened at the Battle of Big Dry Wash. Even historians disagree about where the battle took place. The following is the account given by Al Sieber, a noted Indian scout at the time, and is repeated in *Rim Country History*. Apparently this story is different from the "official" one which, Sieber claims, was written by some junior officer in Washington, D.C., who had never been to Arizona. While facts of this story are suspect, it is nonetheless interesting that it exists.

In July 1882, eighty-six Apache men, women, and children led by Nan-tia-tish escaped from the reservation at Cibique. They killed a Captain Hentig and a few troops while trying to escape. They traveled west through Pleasant Valley, killing two ranchers on the way. When they came to the East Verde River they stopped at the Beluzzi place for supplies. He was away. Some of the Apache went down into Whispering Pines, where John and Margaret Meadows and their children had homesteaded.

When news of the renegade Apaches first spread to the Rim Country, area settlers went into Payson to hole up at the Payson dance hall for protection. John Meadows got tired of waiting and returned with his family to his ranch, believing the Apache wouldn't go there.

Early the next morning John heard his horses snorting and ran outside with his rifle to investigate. His two oldest sons followed him. John was shot before he could get off the porch. Both boys were hit, Henry dying two weeks later. John Jr. was shot in the groin and had to have his leg amputated. The Apache were kept away from the house by Margaret and a younger son, who kept up a steady barrage of bullets, while daughter Eva reloaded. John Sr. was the first man buried at the Payson Pioneer Cemetery.

Al Sieber, Major Chaffee, forty soldiers, and forty Apache scouts chased the escapees up the East Verde River to the top of the Rim, where they caught up with them. One account of the battle says that there was prolonged fighting in the woods, while another account suggests that the escapees were massacred. At any rate, eighty of the eighty-nine escapees were killed, while only one army man died.

27. Whispering Pines

Highlights: Great area for undirected exploring

Seasons: Spring through fall

Distance: 6.2 miles

Time: 2 hours

Difficulty Rating: Easy

High Elevation: 5,660 feet   **Low Elevation:** 5,260 feet

USGS Topographic Maps: Kehl Ridge

Connecting Rides: 24. The Crossings, 25. Control Road West, 26. Washington Park

Access: Follow Arizona 87 2 miles north out of Payson to Houston Mesa Road. Turn right here and follow the road over the rim past the Mesa del Caballo subdivision and the Shoofly Ruins. The road crosses the East Verde River three times and passes through the Whispering Pines subdivision before reaching the steel bridge, about 8 miles past the General Store. (If you are after a strenuous ride, you can start this ride at the Shoofly Ruins.) Start and end at the parking area about 0.3 mile east of the bridge along the left side of the road.

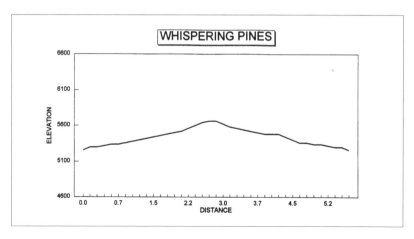

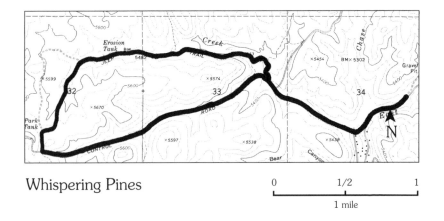

Whispering Pines

```
0          1/2          1
|_____|_____|
         1 mile
```

The Route

Cross back over the bridge, past Houston Mesa Road and FS 32 (1.1 miles), and head up FS 64 to the top of the saddle. There are several false summits as you climb this section but you will know when you come to the top (2.9 miles).

Turn right on FS 438 at the four-way intersection at the top of this saddle. Turn at the next right (3.3 miles) and turn again at the next right you meet (3.8 miles). The road goes in and out of the wash as it descends. There are many side trails here that are excellent for exploring. Just be sure to come back to this wash and keep heading downhill. The wash eventually dumps you back on Control Road (FS 64, 5.2 miles). Follow it back east to your car.

THE HIDDEN FORESTS

Lying between the Diamond Rim and the Mogollon Rim, this area is laced with shallow canyons called "draws" that often hold water. The hills are covered with ponderosa pines. One hundred years ago the many natural meadows here were thick with tall grass. This became a prime area for ranchers, for everything they needed was right at hand.

The ranchers moved into the draws and ran huge herds of cattle, perhaps as many as ten times the number of cattle that are permitted to graze here today. They built schools, churches, sawmills, and corrals. During the 1950s and 1960s, ranchers began to transfer their land to private owners. Many of the old ranches were sold and this area is now a prime spot for summer vacation homes.

The Hidden Forests border the site of one of the most destructive fires in history. The 1990 Dude Fire destroyed thousands of acres of forest, scores of cabins, and killed six firefighters.

The slopes laid bare by the fire eroded quickly and were ravaged by the winter floods of 1992–93. Thousands of tons of debris washed down into the draws, and what were once quiet streamlets are now wide highways of water-washed boulders and rocks.

28. Control Road East

Highlights: Connecting ride for many rides in the Hidden Forests

Seasons: All year, except after a snowstorm

Distance: 8.8 miles

Time: 2.5 hours

Difficulty Rating: Moderate

High Elevation: 5,880 feet   **Low Elevation:** 5,663 feet

USGS Topographic Maps: Promontory Butte, Diamond Point

Connecting Rides: 22. Over the Diamond Rim, 23. Gilliland Gap, 29. South Tonto Village, 30. Tonto Village Forest Loop, 31. Logging Country, 32. Roberts Draw, 33. Mead Ranch, 34. Diamond Point, 35. Pyeatt Draw, 36. Campsite

Access: Head east on Arizona 260 15 miles until you come to the turn for Tonto Village on the west side of the road. Turn left and follow the pavement until it ends at Tonto Village. Start and end here, but be sure not to park on private property.

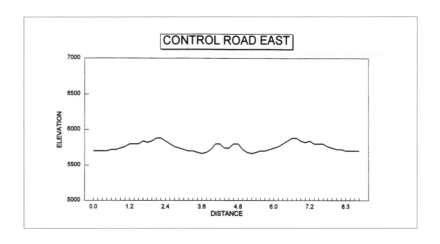

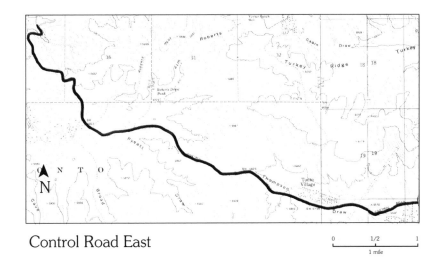

Control Road East

0   1/2   1

1 mile

The Route

Go down the main dirt road to your left at the entrance to Tonto Village. Don't go into the village itself. Climb over a hill at the end of the development and go down the wide, washboard road, past the Diamond Point and Mead Ranch turns (3.6 miles).

Climb up a steep hill after the Diamond Point turn and rapidly descend the other side, past the FS 198 intersection, until you come to Ellison Creek (4.5 miles). The road beyond here passes through the Dude Creek burn area, so this makes a good spot to turn around.

Notes

The road is heavily traveled by vehicles. I recommend this ride only as a means to get to one of the other rides in this area without driving.

 **29. South Tonto Village**

Highlights: Powerline clearing

Seasons: All year, except after a snowstorm

Distance: 2 miles

Time: 1/2-hour

Difficulty Rating: Easy

High Elevation: 5,860 feet   **Low Elevation:** 5,720 feet

USGS Topographic Maps: Diamond Point

Connecting Rides: 28. Control Road East, 30. Tonto Village Forest Loop

Access: Head east on Arizona 260 15 miles until you come to the turn for Tonto Village on the west side of the road. Turn left and follow the paved road until it ends at Tonto Village. Start and end here, but be sure not to park on private property.

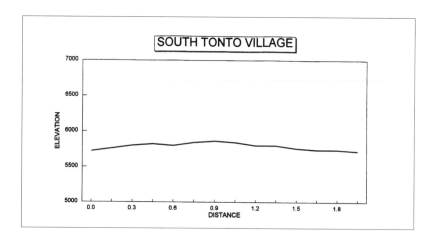

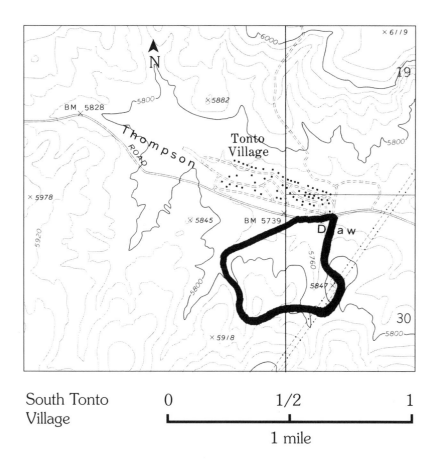

South Tonto
Village

| 0 | 1/2 | 1 |

1 mile

The Route

Look for FS 364 directly across the road to the south of Tonto
Village. Climb up this road into the clearing for the powerlines. Ride
past the clearing and then turn right at the powerlines (0.4 mile).

Climb up the other side of the clearing and onto a jeep trail. This
trail used to go over the Diamond Rim, but it is not maintained now.
You may have to lift your bike over some logs. At the top of the little
wash (0.9 mile) turn right and bomb back down the hill. You will
come out about where you started.

30. Tonto Village Forest Loop

Highlights: Storybook version of what a forest should be
Seasons: All year, except after a snowstorm
Distance: 6 miles
Time: 1.5 hours
Difficulty Rating: Moderate
High Elevation: 5,880 feet   **Low Elevation:** 5,700 feet
USGS Topographic Maps: Diamond Point
Connecting Rides: 28. Control Road East, 29. South Tonto Village,
31. Logging Country, 32. Roberts Draw, 33. Mead Ranch

Access: Drive east on Arizona 260 15 miles until you come to the turn
for Tonto Village on the west side of the road. Turn left and follow the
pavement until it ends at Tonto Village. Start and end here, but be
sure not to park on private property.

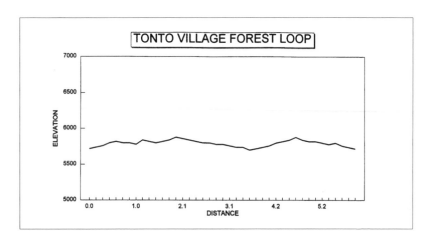

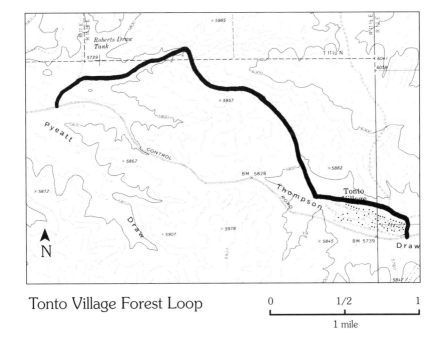

Tonto Village Forest Loop

0   1/2   1

1 mile

The Route

Head north just this side of the houses. Look for a trail heading off to your left. Don't take the one close to the houses; take the next one. Follow it along behind the housing development to your left (0.6 mile).

Pass under two sets of powerlines, then come to an intersection just after a small wash. The trail to the left leads over a small hill, then back to the Control Road. Take the trail to the right, up the wash (1.5 miles). The trail becomes narrower and poorly defined as you get to the saddle. It will look as though you should turn left here, but go straight ahead, down the wash.

At first the trail is gone and you will be riding in a wash. The trail comes out of the wash on the right after a few dozen yards. It then drops into a wide wash. Follow it downstream. The trail may be indistinct.

When you come to an intersection, turn left and head downhill to Control Road (FS 64, 3.6 miles). Turn left and follow Control Road back over the hill to Tonto Village.

Notes

The Haught family had a ranch and a small sawmill here. The sawmill was used irregularly so it was bought and sold a number of times over the years.

 # 31. Logging Country

Highlights: Turn any way you want

Seasons: All year, except after a snowstorm

Distance: 2.2 miles

Time: 1/2-hour

Difficulty Rating: Very easy

High Elevation: 5,980 feet   **Low Elevation:** 5,780 feet

USGS Topographic Maps: Diamond Point

Connecting Rides: 28. Control Road East

Access: Drive east on Arizona 260 15 miles until you come to the turn for Tonto Village on the west side of the road. Turn left and follow the pavement until it ends at Tonto Village, then take Control Road over the hill. Look for the first road to your left after you pass the "Road Closed" sign to your right.

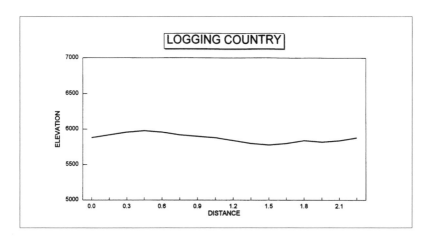

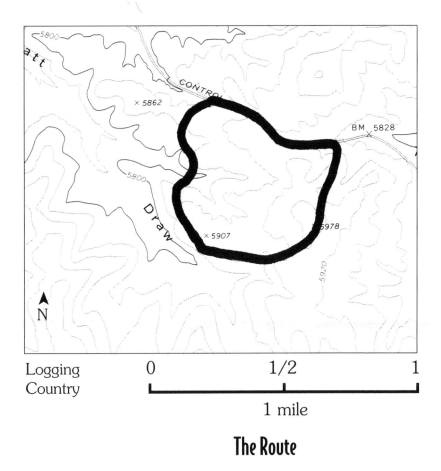

Logging
Country

0   1/2   1

1 mile

The Route

Head uphill and take the first left (0.7 mile). Take the next left to get back to the road. That's it!

Notes

This ride is located in a maze of old logging roads. They are not too steep or rocky so they are easy to climb and a blast to come down. All of the roads connect to the Control Road (FS 64) so you can wander around in here for hours without getting lost or tired of riding. Just head back downhill when you are ready to quit. Great ride for first-timers or if you just want to fool around on your bike.

 # 32. Roberts Draw

Highlights: Long Ranch, some single track

Seasons: All year, except after a snowstorm

Distance: 8 miles

Time: 2.5 hours

Difficulty Rating: Difficult

High Elevation: 6,080 feet   **Low Elevation:** 5,700 feet

USGS Topographic Maps: Diamond Point

Connecting Rides: 28. Control Road East, 29. South Tonto Village, 30. Tonto Village Forest Loop, 31. Logging Country, 33. Mead Ranch

Access: Drive east on Arizona 260 15 miles until you come to the turn for Tonto Village on the west side of the road. Turn left and follow the pavement until it ends at Tonto Village. Start and end here, but be sure not to park on private property.

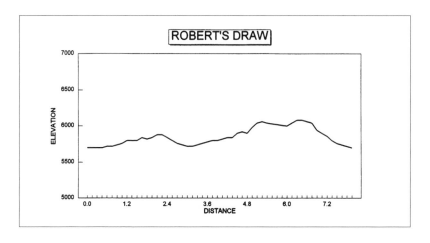

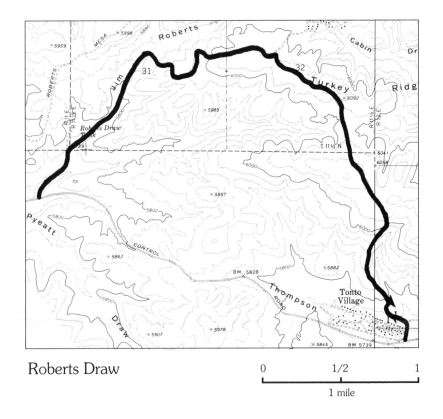

Roberts Draw

```
0              1/2              1
├──────────────┼──────────────┤
        1 mile
```

The Route

Follow the Control Road East ride description (see page 138). Go 3.1 miles until you get to a road on the right marked "primitive and unsuitable for vehicles" (3.1 miles). If you come to the Mead Ranch Road, you have gone too far. You can also follow the Tonto Village Forest Loop description (see page 142) until you come to Control Road.

Turn to the north on the "primitive" road and follow the draw upstream. Turn left at the first intersection (3.3 miles), then turn right at the next intersection (3.4 miles). Follow this trail as it climbs up the wash until it is blocked off by a barbed wire fence (4.2 miles).

Please do not enter the private property beyond the fence. Instead, you can turn to the right on a faint trail. This trail climbs up and away from the wash. Near the top of this climb the road is blocked by a water bar (4.6 miles). Go around it and then turn to the left. The trail to the right looks good, but it dead-ends in a forest.

The road drops down into another wash and then passes through a gate. Climb the hill and go to the left for a fast descent.

Suddenly you will come out of the forest to meet a wide dirt road (6 miles). Turn right. The road to the left is the old, back way into Mead Ranch. Just a few yards past this intersection, another road comes in from the left. Ignore it and ride straight ahead, up and over the hill.

When you come off this hill be careful because it is steep, rocky, and full of ruts. The many side trails are good for exploring; they mostly dead-end after a bit and are blocked to motor vehicle use by the Forest Service.

Look for your car at the bottom.

Notes

Myrtle Point, on the Rim above this ride, is named for the young daughter of Elwood "Grandad" Pyle, who died near there. (See notes to Washington Park, page 132–134.)

Elam Boles was an enterprising man who ran a mule pack train between Tonto Basin and Fort McDowell. He eventually tired of this business and sold it for $75, which he used to buy Mead Ranch. Boles was sweet on a widow in Payson and her two young sons. She wouldn't agree to marry him, though, until he built a new house for the family. The house was built and the ranch occupied by the new family.

 # 33. Mead Ranch

Highlights: Dude Fire Scenic Drive

Seasons: All year, except after a snowstorm

Distance: 13.1 miles

Time: 4 hours

Difficulty Rating: Difficult

High Elevation: 6,100 feet   **Low Elevation:** 5,663 feet

USGS Topographic Maps: Diamond Point, Promontory Butte

Connecting Rides: 28. Control Road East, 29. South Tonto Village, 30. Tonto Village Forest Loop, 31. Logging Country, 32. Roberts Draw, 34. Diamond Point, 35. Pyeatt Draw, 36. Campsite, 39. Tonto Creek

Access: Head east on Arizona 260 15 miles until you come to the turn for Tonto Village on the west side of the road. Turn left and follow the pavement until it ends at Tonto Village.

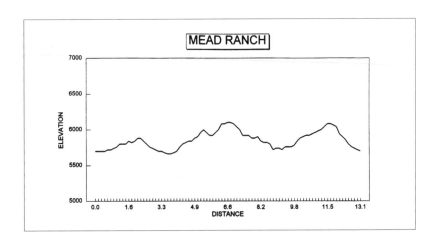

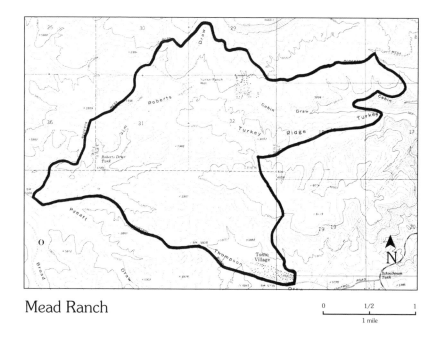

Mead Ranch

0   1/2   1

1 mile

The Route

Follow the route description for Control Road East (see page 138). After 3.5 miles you come to the turn for Mead Ranch. There is a sign here explaining the start of the Dude Fire Scenic Drive. Turn right. Look for the numbered scenic drive markers along the way.

Once you get to the top of the hill you can see the Dude Fire destruction on Roberts Mesa directly ahead of you. The road drops down into Roberts Draw and to your right you can see where firefighters fought to save the ranch. Climb out of Roberts Draw up the barren hill straight ahead.

At the top of the mesa you will return to forest just as you reach the turn to Mead Ranch, to your right (7.5 miles). The road becomes much rougher here as you continue straight ahead.

As you come off the mesa, look to your right for the FS 29A sign (8.2 miles). Turn onto the road, just this side of the barbed wire fence.

The road is level for a couple of yards, then drops steeply into Cabin Draw. Halfway into the draw the road splits (8.8 miles). Take the road to your right that leads back up into the draw. The road to your left dead-ends at the powerlines.

The road ascends gently as you head back up the wash and then crosses over to the other side (9.5 miles). You will be climbing more steeply now, heading back out to the ridge line where the road is blocked off by huge boulders (9.8 miles). Turn right here.

The road climbs up the ridge, leveling off occasionally, giving your climbing legs a break. Near the top of the hill the road meets a T-intersection (11.2 miles). Turn left. (The road to the right is the old way back to Mead Ranch.)

Climb a little bit longer over this hill. Once on the other side the road descends steeply. You will need to use your brakes here. There are a number of dead-end side trails leading off this road that are good for exploring. The Forest Service has blocked all of them off to motor vehicles with water bars, so the trails are in varying states of decay. Stick to the main road and soon you will be back to your car.

Notes

The following information corresponds to numbered markers you pass along this ride. Details come from the Tonto National Forest Self-Guided Auto Tour of the Dude Fire. Look for the markers as you ride. There is additional information in the notes section of the Campsite ride (see page 161) as well as in the history section at the front of the book (see pages 13–14).

1) This is what the forest looked like before the 1990 fire. Notice the thick undergrowth and the accumulation of dead logs.

2) Good view of the Rim from here. The Rim catches the moist air heading in from the south and pushes it aloft, forming clouds. The Rim creates its own weather. Lightning caused by an over-the-Rim thunderstorm started the Dude Fire.

3) This is a fire control line. Bulldozers scrape the earth down to the mineral soil, hoping to keep the blaze from crossing the line.

4) In many places fire destroyed all the vegetation that holds the topsoil in place. Soon after the fire, torrential rains washed away one and one-half inches of topsoil. Crews worked feverishly to replant the area to conserve as much of the soil as possible. They were aided by

A Forest Service marker describes the Dude Fire Scenic Drive.

aerial seeding. Fences were repaired as soon as possible to keep cattle from eating the tender new plants.

5) This area was totally destroyed by the fire. The burned trees will eventually topple over as their roots decay and they lose the power to stand. Lumber and firewood have been sold to get wood that was burned on the outside, but still good on the inside, before it becomes infested with beetles.

6) On the north side of the road the fire burned incredibly hot, causing the sap in the young trees to boil. The raging inferno reduced the forest to ashes. On the south side of the road the fire mainly burned the undergrowth, benefitting the forest by stimulating the growth of grasses and other plants that animals eat.

7) This is a siltation device. They were built right after the fire to prevent damage to roads and culverts from rocks, stumps, and logs that would wash down from the burned-out area.

8) The fire raged here.

34. Diamond Point

Highlights: Views from Diamond Point and the cave

Seasons: All year, except after a snowstorm

Distance: 8.8 miles

Time: 3 hours

Difficulty Rating: Moderate

High Elevation: 6,380 feet   **Low Elevation:** 5,663 feet

USGS Topographic Maps: Diamond Point

Connecting Rides: 28. Control Road East

Access: Follow Arizona 260 east 15 miles to the turnoff for Tonto Village on the west side of the road. Turn left and follow Control Road for about 3.5 miles until you come to the turnoff for Diamond Point.

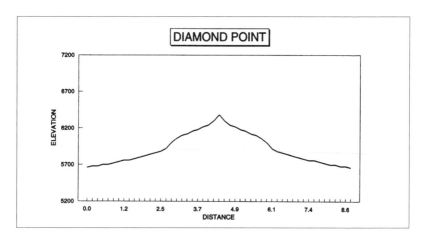

The Route

Follow the wide road uphill through Broad Draw. The road is fairly well-maintained and you should be able to climb easily. At the

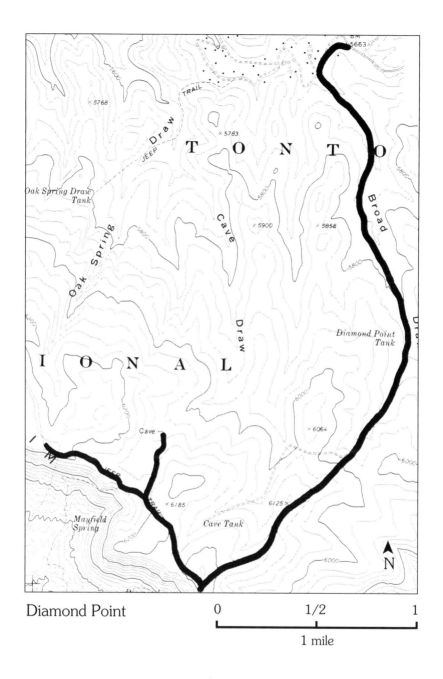

Diamond Point

0   1/2   1

1 mile

edge of the Rim you will come to a fence (3.4 miles). Beyond the fence is Diamond Point itself, with its radio towers and fire lookout. The gate is usually locked, but you may find it open during fire season. The views from here are spectacular.

The trail you want begins a few yards back down the road, where the road first climbs onto the ridge top. Follow the trail to the north as it enters the woods and crosses a small wash. You will cross over another small hill and then begin descending.

Watch for the cave trail to your right (4.0 miles). Ride down to an open meadow. The cave is in the middle of a clearing in what looks like flat ground (4.4 miles).

The cave looks like a crack in the earth that drops down about fifteen feet. I am told that the real cave entrance is about halfway down the pit in the side. It is a technical entrance that requires quite a bit of wriggling to get into.

Return up to the trail along the Rim. If you are interested in more views you can turn right here. There is an old overgrown trail off the west side of the Rim, but reports are that this road is incredibly steep and overgrown. You can continue along the Rim for about another 0.5 mile, when the road finally dies out.

Return along the same route.

Notes

Rock crystals here are called Arizona Diamonds and were traded extensively by Native Americans.

There are a number of caves located in limestone regions of the Rim Country. Cavers who know and explore these caverns try to keep the locations secret from the public and government agencies. They share information only with fellow spelunkers to help protect these fragile environments.

 # 35. Pyeatt Draw

Highlights: Parklike settings along Ellison Creek

Seasons: All year, except after snowstorms

Distance: 9.2 miles

Time: 3 hours

Difficulty Rating: Moderate

High Elevation: 5,740 feet   **Low Elevation:** 5,260 feet

USGS Topographic Maps: Diamond Point

Connecting Rides: 22. Over the Diamond Rim, 23. Gilliland Gap, 28. Control Road East

Access: Follow Arizona 260 east 15 miles to the turnoff for Tonto Village on the west side of the road. Turn left and follow Control Road for about 4.5 miles until you come to the turn for FS 198 on the left. Start and end here.

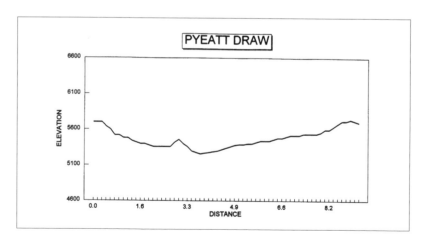

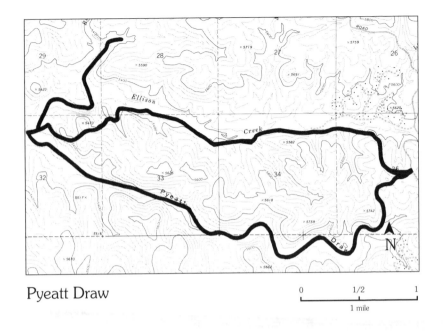

Pyeatt Draw

0   1/2   1

1 mile

The Route

Follow the signed FS 198 road downhill to the west along the beautiful parklike Ellison Creek for the next 3 miles. The creek bed is in the trees just off to your right. The road is wide and well-maintained so you can really fly if you wish.

The road goes up a big hill and you will lose the stream for a while. The descent from this hill is quick as it takes you back to the creek bottom (3.6 miles). To your right, just before you get into the creek bottom, is a small trail that you may want to explore.

If so, follow this trail back up the Ellison Creek bottom until you come to a fence on the other side of the wash. Instead of going through the gate, take the trail to your left. Climb up the hill and drop back into the wash, Perly Creek. You will notice ever-increasing evidence of the 1990 Dude Fire as you head up this section, until you are finally blocked off by numerous burned and downed trees. Turn around here and head back to the main road (FS 193). Turn right,

Evidence of the destructive Dude Fire along Perly Creek.

then quickly turn left into Pyeatt Draw. The trail crosses the wash and then climbs gently, crossing the creek a couple of times before coming to a T-intersection (5.5 miles).

Turn left at the T, cross the creek, then immediately turn right and head once again up the wash. The trail is a little more difficult to pick out here and even appears to end. You may have to push once in a while. Eventually, look for another trail crossing the creek and another intersection (7.6 miles). Turn left here.

Quickly cross the creek twice on this road until you come to another intersection (8.0 miles). The better road to the right leads back to the Diamond Point summer homes. Take the left-hand turn and go up the hill past a stock tank. The trail drops you back down to the right and to your car.

Notes

Colonel J. W. "Jessie" Ellison was a southern gentleman who owned a plantation in the Deep South. At the end of the Civil War he worried about losing everything to carpetbaggers from the North, so he moved his family to Texas and took up ranching. He had some prime land there and fenced it off with the newly invented barbed wire. His neighbors were continually cutting through his fences so that they could get to the good watering holes. By 1885 he grew tired of fixing fences and decided to move his whole operation to central Arizona. He boarded eighteen hundred cattle, two hundred horses, and all of the ranching and household supplies he and his family owned on a train and shipped it all to Bowie, Arizona, the depot nearest to the Rim Country. The cattle stampeded as soon as they were let off the train and it took several days to gather them all up. The Colonel, his family, and some hired hands took thirty days to drive the entire herd to Safford, and another thirty days to get to Globe. By that time winter was setting in, so they decided to winter in a valley where the Tonto Creek met the Salt River, now under Roosevelt Lake. The cattle were able to recover there and fatten up some, too. In spring they drove the herd the rest of the way to the Rim Country, settling along what is now Ellison Creek. They built a home and called it Apple Valley. This ranch became the center of activity for the region for a while, even needing a post office for a couple of years. A school was opened in 1889.

Ellison was good to the people who helped him get the cattle to his new ranch. He gave some of his cattle to Rance Moore, who settled on what became known as Moore Creek. This creek comes into Ellison Creek across the wash from the road about halfway down to the turn into Pyeatt Draw.

Perly Creek is named for Ellison's oldest son, Pearl.

 # 36. Campsite

Highlights: Great views at the start of this ride

Seasons: All year, except after a snowstorm

Distance: 3.3 miles

Time: 1 hour

Difficulty Rating: Easy

High Elevation: 5,920 feet   **Low Elevation:** 5,660 feet

USGS Topographic Maps: Diamond Point

Connecting Rides: 28. Control Road East, 33. Mead Ranch, 34. Diamond Point

Access: Follow Arizona 260 east 15 miles to the turnoff for Tonto Village on the west side of the road. Turn left and follow Control Road for about 4 miles. Go past the turn for Diamond Point and up the hill. Park at the camping spot with a great view on the right side of the road.

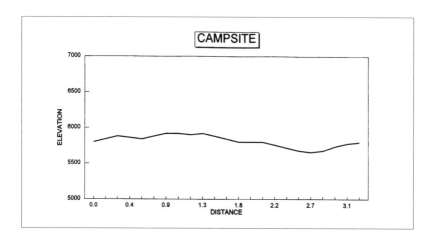

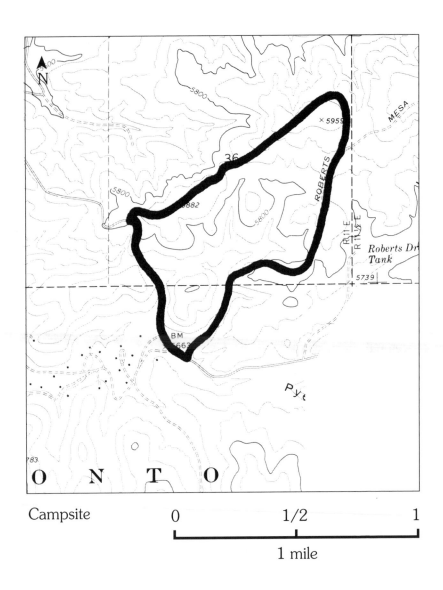

Campsite

0   1/2   1

1 mile

The Hidden Forests

The Route

The trail takes off to your right from here and climbs the hill. Follow the fence line at the top of the hill. Drop down a bit and then go back up and through the gate (0.7 mile). Follow the main trail as it turns to the right at an intersection (1.2 miles). When you come out onto Mead Ranch Road, turn right (1.5 miles). You can bomb down this hill. Turn right at Control Road (2.5 miles), then climb back up the steep hill to your car. Easy, isn't it?

Notes

I named this route Campsite because it looks as though a lot of people think this is a good place to car camp. This spot also provides a good view of the Dude Fire burn area.

Dude Fire started on June 25, 1990, when lightning struck the unusually dry forest and touched off a blaze. The temperature was hot, the humidity was low, the forest was full of fuel, and there had been several years of very low precipitation. Within hours the fire was a raging inferno.

Fire crews rushed to contain the fire, but it took over ten days to control it. The fire was fought on the ground and from the air. Eventually, over 2,600 people worked to contain the fire. Fourteen helicopters, 14 water tenders, 10 air tankers, 12 bulldozers, and 33 fire engines were called out. Over 24,000 acres were burned to one degree or another and 1,153 people were evacuated. Sadly, 6 firefighters were killed and scores of summer homes destroyed. For more information see the notes section of Mead Ranch (page 150) and the comments about fires in the introduction (pages 13–14).

THE HIGH CANYONS

The rides in this area are located where the mountains are high and the canyons deep. The steep slopes are covered with ponderosa pine and the canyons usually have streams in them. To the south, the Sierra Ancha Mountains rise up to the edge of the Rim.

The granite here is very hard, which makes for some technical riding. Canyons near the Rim are also filled with sedimentary rock that has washed down during storms.

These canyons used to be the only way to access the Rim Country from the east. Still today, Highway 260 is one of the few paved roads to cross the Rim for hundreds of miles.

37. Little Green Valley

Highlights: Little Green Valley

Seasons: All year, except after snowstorms

Distance: 7 miles

Time: 2 hours

Difficulty Rating: Easy

High Elevation: 5,700 feet **Low Elevation:** 5,300 feet

USGS Topographic Maps: Diamond Point, Promontory Butte

Access: Follow Arizona 260 east from Payson 13 miles to Ponderosa Campground. Park at the entrance.

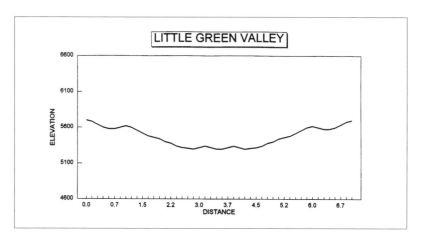

The Route

Head straight down the main campground road until you get to the far end. The road is blocked to motor vehicles by a large gate, but you will be able to walk right under it. Turn right at the dirt road just past the gate (0.7 mile).

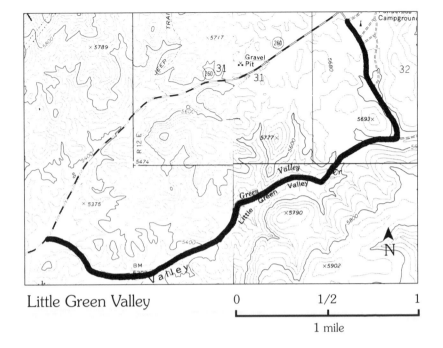

Little Green Valley

0   1/2   1

1 mile

This road will carry you down gradually through a thick ponderosa pine forest to Little Green Valley. Pass a marked trailhead leading to the Hell's Gate Wilderness (2.5 miles).

After the trailhead the route goes over a small hill and drops into Little Green Valley (3.5 miles). Turn around here.

Notes

This area was originally settled in 1876 by William Burch and John Hood, who were attracted to the lush, chest-high grass in the meadow. After a couple of years Hood stayed at the ranch while Burch moved into Payson. Payson was sometimes called Big Green Valley so Hood referred to his ranch as the Little Green Valley.

Hell's Gate Wilderness is named after the cattle trail that led from the Little Green Valley to Young, where cattle were driven over the Rim on the Crooked Trail to Holbrook (see the notes section of Gentry

Giant Loop, pages 228–229). Hell's Gate is named for where the trail crosses Tonto Creek deep in a canyon surrounded by sheer rock walls.

In 1918 the Haught School opened for children living in the Little Green Valley. The schoolhouse was located above the ranch house across from where this ride enters the meadow. This school was attended almost exclusively by children of the Haught family until it was closed in 1935.

38. Bear Flats

Highlights: Tonto Creek

Seasons: All year, except after a snowstorm

Distance: 8.4 miles

Time: 3 hours

Difficulty Rating: Difficult

High Elevation: 5,680 fee   **Low Elevation:** 4,940 feet

USGS Topographic Maps: Promontory Butte

Connecting Rides: 28. Control Road East, 37. Little Green Valley

Access: Travel east on Arizona 260 15 miles. Look for the turnoff to Bear Flats on the right side of the road just past Ponderosa Campground. Park at the dirt turnout just off the highway.

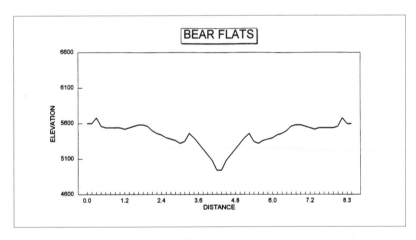

The Route

Ride down through some open meadows. Go left at the first intersection (1.0 miles).

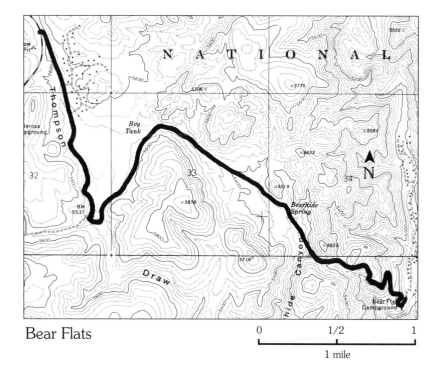

Bear Flats

```
0              1/2              1
├──────────────┼──────────────┤
           1 mile
```

The road climbs up through a saddle before it begins its perilous descent into the canyon, switchbacking several times. At the canyon bottom is an old campground (4.2 miles). Across the creek from here is the Hell's Gate Wilderness. The Hell's Gate itself is a couple of miles down the creek from here. Across the creek is the Bear Flats subdivision. Turn around here and head back the way you came in.

Notes

Bear Flats is named for the black bears who visit the area, attracted by the berries here.

 # 39. Tonto Creek

Highlights: Tonto Creek, fish hatchery

Seasons: Spring through fall

Distance: 12.4 miles

Time: 3 hours

Difficulty Rating: Difficult

High Elevation: 6,360 feet   **Low Elevation:** 5,360 feet

USGS Topographic Maps: Promontory Butte, Knoll Lake

Connecting Rides: 33. Mead Ranch, 40. Horton Springs

Access: Travel east on Arizona 260 15 miles to Kohl's Ranch. You can park here or head north up FS 289 into the Tonto Creek area and park at the Horton Creek picnic area. Mileage distances are measured from Kohl's Ranch. This ride will loop you back to your car.

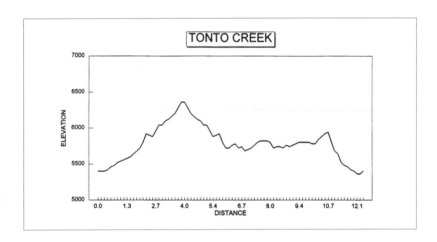

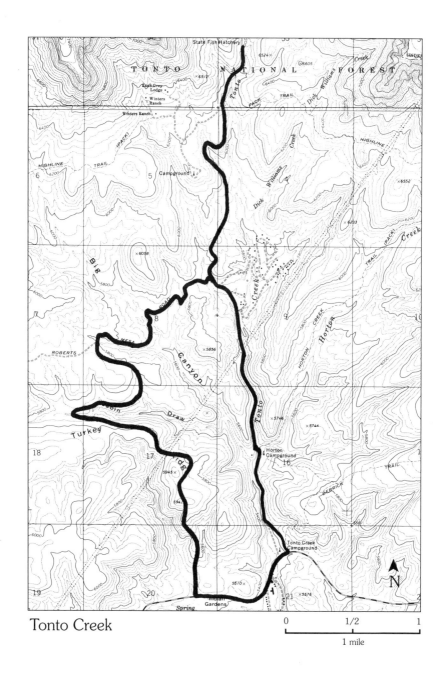

Tonto Creek

0   1/2   1

1 mile

N

The Route

You may feel that this is not an "authentic" mountain bike ride since it starts on a paved road, but the Tonto Creek is a beautiful place to ride and the last half of this ride is very rugged.

Head up the paved road past the campgrounds and picnic areas. There are numerous good wading pools in the creek along here. The road branches away from the creek at the Baptist Camp turnoff. Watch for the dirt road to your left as you climb the hill. You will be taking this one on the way back down.

The road climbs steeply and then contours around the side of the hill, rejoining the creek. Look for the Zane Grey Estates turn near the top of this hill and continue on to the fish hatchery, where the road dead-ends.

Return back down the paved road and turn onto FS 29 at the sign. Don't fly by it on the way down. The dirt road crosses a deep wash and is partially washed away. It climbs another hill and then drops quickly into Big Canyon (6.9 miles). The road gets rougher beyond this point. Ignore the numerous side trails through here.

Ascend Roberts Mesa into a clearing. This is the site of an old forest fire. Look for a fence and a road just past it to your left, FS 29A (7.6 miles). There should be a sign here. Follow FS 29A into the canyon.

Halfway into the draw the road splits (8.2 miles). Take the road to your right back up into the draw. Head back up the wash and then cross over to the other side (8.9 miles). Ride back out to the ridge line where the road is blocked off by some huge boulders (9.4 miles). Head straight past the boulders and continue to climb the ridge until you get to the powerline clearing (10.0 miles).

Go left here and curve around the south side of the hill by a tank. The road twists back to the right and climbs steeply up the hill. The top of the hill is flat (10.7 miles). Things start to get tricky here. The road goes straight ahead but dead-ends down in a thick pine forest. Look for the highest point of the hill to your right. There used to be a road leading out to the edge, but it has been blocked by falling trees and is now overgrown. But don't panic. Once you reach the high point of the hill, look for an opening in the manzanitas to your left.

One of the sites along Tonto Creek.

If it looks like a rockslide leading straight down, you have found the route. You will have to slide with your bike down here, but the trail levels out after a bit and you should be able to start riding. When you come to a fence line (11.3 miles), turn right. This is Indian Gardens. Head out to Highway 260 (11.6 miles) and hang a left. Take the highway back to your car.

Notes

Kohl's Ranch was settled in 1884 by Mr. and Mrs. Dellbridge and their five children. The ranch changed hands a couple of times, eventually ending up with Lewis and Neecie Cole in 1924. They established a guest ranch here, and it had a post office from 1939 to 1974. The present buildings were built in the mid-1960s.

The lower Tonto Creek campground near the highway was the site of Boy Scout Camp Geronimo before it was moved west to its present location on Webber Creek.

The Tonto Creek was named by King S. Woolsey on his expedition in 1864. At first, *Tonto Apache* was a name used to describe all of the Apache in Arizona, but the Apache themselves began to apply the word *Tonto* to the more settled tribes of the Rim Country. Tonto carried a negative connotation because the tribe was looked down upon by settlers and other Apache groups. (The tribes of this region were given the name *Tantos* on an 1820 map, so Tonto might be a corruption of this earlier term.)

The creek joining the Tonto at the Baptist Camp is called Dick Williams after an early ranger who lived there.

Anderson Lee "Babe" Haught was persuaded by his brother, John, to come to the Rim Country from Texas in the late 1800s. John had visited some of the relatives already living here. They took a train to Maricopa, Arizona, and spent months walking to the Rim Country up the Salt River and Tonto Creek. They settled in a cabin that had been built by some of their relatives on a ranch in what is now the Zane Grey Estates.

Babe and John both married and started families. They built a bigger cabin on the property in 1910, but John and his family eventually moved to Winslow. Babe became an accomplished hunter and traveled widely throughout the Rim Country. When Zane Grey came to Payson after the publication of his first novel, he stayed at the cabin and Babe guided him on many hunting trips. The family provided information for several of Grey's novels. Grey purchased three acres of land from Babe and had him build a cabin. Grey came to the cabin often to hunt and to write. Unfortunately, the cabin burned down in the 1990 Dude Fire.

The fish hatchery was built as a WPA project in the 1930s about four hundred yards below Tonto Springs. Initially, a string of ponds was dug out here and a piping system built to keep them supplied with water. Several cabins were built to house hatchery workers. The hatchery was rebuilt in 1987 as the state-of-the-art facility you see now. The tents protect the fish from the sun and keep the water from becoming too hot. The building houses the egg hatching tanks and a small museum.

The hillside at the FS 29A turnoff was burned in 1961. Ironically, this area has stopped the spread of several forest fires since then because the trees now growing are spaced far apart and have very little undergrowth. Most of the trees here were planted in the 1970s.

Early Native Americans grew crops at the present-day spring-fed Indian gardens up to the early 1900s.

 # 40. Horton Springs

Highlights: Horton Springs

Seasons: Spring through fall

Distance: 7 miles

Time: 2 hours

Difficulty Rating: Difficult

High Elevation: 6,740 fee   **Low Elevation:** 5,440 feet

USGS Topographic Maps: Promontory Butte

Connecting Rides: 39. Tonto Creek

Access: Travel east on Arizona 260 15 miles to Tonto Creek. Turn left on Tonto Creek Road and follow it for about 1 mile and park at the Horton Creek picnic area.

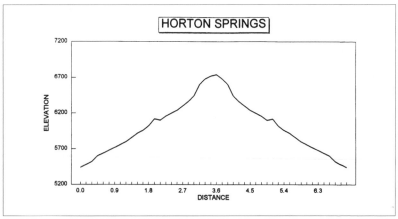

The Route

Cross the bridge over Tonto Creek and head up the campground road. The trailhead is marked with a sign just before you get into the campground. Follow Horton Creek Trail 285.

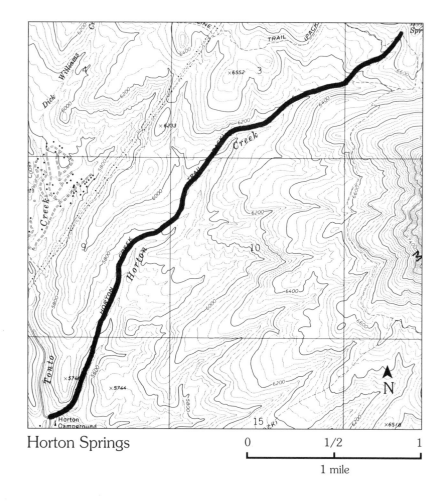

Horton Springs

0   1/2   1

1 mile

Head down the hill and cross Horton Creek, here just a dry creek bed. Follow the road up the hill and through a gate. After a few dozen yards there is another fence line and two gates. Take the trail to the right for a bit of single-track riding. Be careful, though, as this is a popular hiking area, too. Please don't give cyclists a bad name by being obnoxious on this trail. After about 0.25 mile the trail rejoins the road.

The road climbs steadily up the canyon and gradually deteriorates. It is *very* rocky and difficult to ride in places. The canyon walls narrow the higher you climb. The trail makes one switchback high in the canyon, then rejoins the creek near the springs. The Highline Trail intersects here. A fence protects the springs from cattle. Turn around here and take the road all the way back down.

Notes

Horton Creek offers a fine example of Arizona stream geology. The springs are formed from rainwater that collects on top of the Rim. The rocks along the Rim act as a giant sponge, soaking up water. But at this level there is a layer of rock that does not soak up water. Now, imagine a saturated sponge on top of a kitchen counter. As more water is added to the top, like rain on the Rim, the sponge leaks out water on the counter, like Horton Springs.

As the stream flows down the hill it stays on top of the rocks. A little farther down the creek the rock layer becomes porous again and a lot of loose debris fills the creek. At that point the stream disappears. This is why you see flowing water at the top of this ride, but not at the bottom.

The creek is named for Willis B. Horton of Mississippi who lived halfway up this canyon. The pools at the top of the canyon are the site of the first fish hatchery in the Rim Country.

 # 41. Christopher Mountain

Highlights: "Top of the Hill" riding

Seasons: Spring through fall

Distance: 15 miles

Time: 4 hours

Difficulty Rating: Difficult

High Elevation: 6,860 feet   **Low Elevation:** 5,980 feet

USGS Topographic Maps: Woods Canyon, Promontory Butte

Connecting Rides: 42. Two-Sixty Trailhead

Access: Follow Arizona 260 east about 24 miles, passing Christopher Creek. Look for the Colcord Road turnoff across from the highway maintenance yard just before the highway widens to four lanes and begins to climb the hill. Turn right onto Colcord Road and take it to the top of the hill, about 0.5 mile. There are a number of logging roads here so the one you want may be hard to find. It is right at the top of the hill.

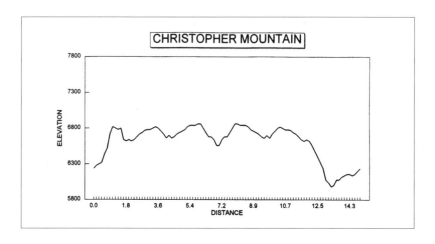

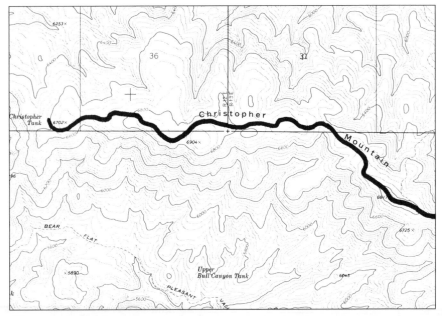

Christopher Mountain

The Route

Head up the mountain to the west. You will know you have found the right road if you pass through a gate about 20 yards from Colcord Road. The trail is very steep here. At the intersection (0.7 mile), a good-looking trail heads off to the left while a nastier-looking trail goes right. Take the nasty-looking trail. This trail climbs steeply up the mountain, then winds around to the north side, crossing a number of water bars, before it drops steeply to a much smoother road (1.8 miles). Turn left on this road.

This area has been extensively logged, so it is quite open. The road follows the top of the mountain to the west. There are a number of small ups and downs along here. Even though you are at the top of the mountain, there are few good views. All along the top you will pass a number of side trails that the Forest Service has blocked off with water bars. Stick to the main road.

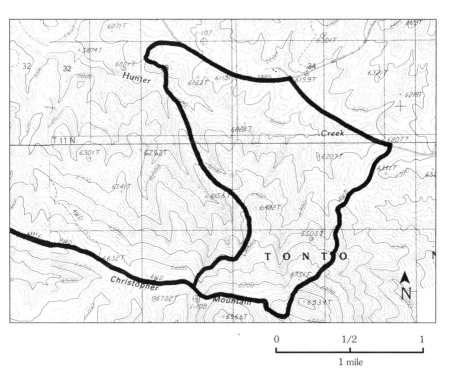

```
0          1/2          1
└──────────┴──────────┘
        1 mile
```

Look for a large stock tank with a small dam and concrete spill-way to the right of the main trail (5.5 miles). The road goes through a gate and suddenly becomes steeper and rockier. This jeep road de-scends quite steeply in places, to another stock tank (6.9 miles). Turn around at the tank. (The trail does continue down a rocky single track to Box Canyon. Local cyclists sometimes turn this ride into a loop, but it is very steep and requires riding several miles on the highway.) Head all the way back to the intersection in the logged area (12.1 miles).

This time, instead of going back the way you came, head down the road to your left. This road is very steep, but not too rocky. There are no uphills to slow your descent, so be careful not to let your speed outpace your ability. When you come to a T-intersection (12.8 miles), take the road to your left down into the canyon. Cross the canyon, then climb out of the wash and continue downhill to Hunter Creek (13.3 miles).

Be careful here, as the creek may have water in it after a rain or snowstorm. The road will tend toward the right as you climb out of the canyon. Once out of the Hunter Creek area the road parallels the highway for a bit before dumping out onto the highway (13.7 miles).

You can follow the highway back to Colcord Road and your car, or you can take your bike through the woods for 0.5 mile along the highway.

 # 42. Two-Sixty Trailhead

Highlights: "The best single track in the state" says Dan Basinski, local mountain bike hero

Seasons: Spring through fall

Distance: 11.5 miles

Time: 3 hours

Difficulty Rating: Moderate

High Elevation: 6,800 feet   **Low Elevation:** 6,120 feet

USGS Topographic Maps: Woods Canyon, Promontory Butte

Connecting Rides: 41. Christopher Mountain

Access: Take Arizona 260 east for about 25 miles. Look for the sign marking the Two-Sixty Trailhead on the west side of the highway, just after it widens to four lanes.

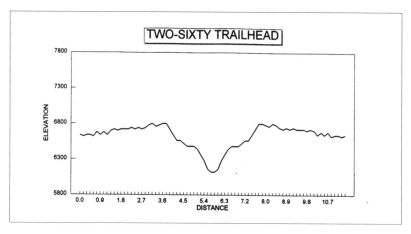

The Route

Start at the Two-Sixty Trailhead, one of many trailheads that access the Highline Trail. It can be rocky at times as it contours around

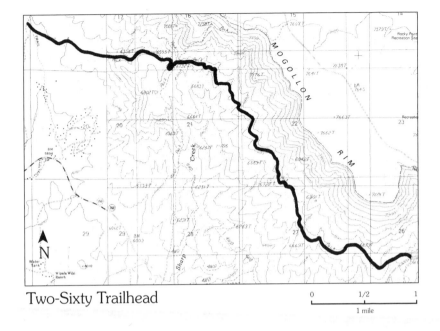

Two-Sixty Trailhead

0	1/2	1

1 mile

the middle of the Rim, descends into drainages, and climbs out to the ridges. There are some technical sections, especially when you go into the drainages.

At 3.7 miles you will come to a gate and a four-way intersection. One sign points uphill for a trail to the Rim. It is a push. Another sign points straight ahead and says Christopher Creek. *Do not take this trail.* You will get to Christopher Creek all right, after 2 miles of riding a rocky, brushy, overgrown, unmaintained trail. For the "best single track in the state," turn left here and follow the trail down to Christopher Creek.

There is a parking lot across the creek from the trail. You can either turn around and go back the way you came, or you can follow the dirt road from the parking lot back to the highway, and then follow the highway east back to your car.

Notes

The creek is named for Isadore Christopher who had a ranch near the present-day hamlet of Christopher Creek. In July 1882,

"The best single track in the state!"

Isadore killed a bear, skinned it, and hung the skin in one of his two cabins. The next day he was away when Apache renegades, escapees from the nearby reservation, burned his two cabins (see notes section of Washington Park, pages 132–134). The troops who were pursuing the renegades arrived at the cabins while they were engulfed in flames. A story spread claiming the troops thought the burned bearhide was the skinned remains of Isadore. The soldiers purportedly gave the burned skin a proper burial.

STAR VALLEY

Granite hills surround this sand-filled valley. The land slopes steeply to the south to the Tonto Creek Canyon and is covered with piñon and juniper woodlands as well as patches of ponderosa pine.

The valley was first settled in 1878 by John Starr, a miner from Belgium. He was killed by Apaches and buried at the ranch site. Various ranchers have used the valley over the years and it became a small population center. There are now a number of houses here. Once separated from Payson by the steep hill between them, the completion of the four-lane highway and the numerous Forest Service land trades have brought Star Valley ever closer to Payson. There are several new housing developments between the communities and it shouldn't be long before the two are joined.

43. Preacher Canyon

Highlights: Preacher Canyon

Seasons: All year

Distance: 6.1 miles

Time: 2 hours

Difficulty Rating: Moderate

High Elevation: 5,080 feet   **Low Elevation:** 4,900 feet

USGS Topographic Maps: Diamond Point

Connecting Rides: 44. Pocket Cabin Trail

Access: Follow Arizona 260 east 9 miles. Look for FS 436 down the canyon to the right.

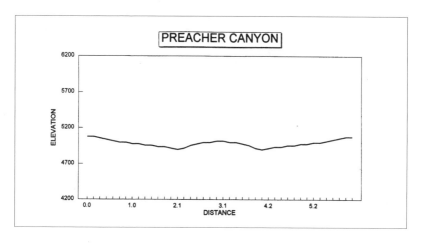

The Route

Cross the wash and ride the smooth road. The canyon is to your left. Pass under some powerlines (0.6 mile) and continue on the main road. Ignore the trails to your right as well as the side road that leads down the canyon under the powerline.

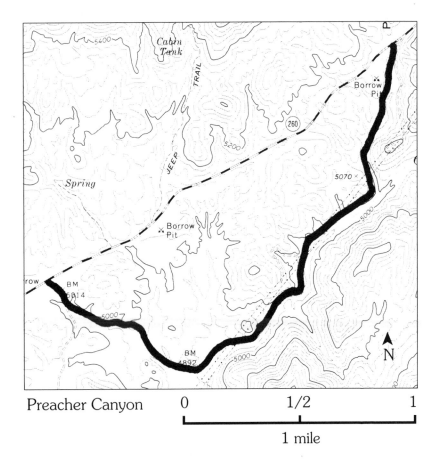

Preacher Canyon

| 0 | 1/2 | 1 |

1 mile

Pass by the transformer station and head up the small hill. Turn around at the highway (3 miles) and return by the same route.

Notes

During the Pleasant Valley War in the 1880s, a preacher lived in this canyon. He didn't want to get involved in the feud, so he always carried a shotgun that he would fire periodically to warn anyone within earshot of his approach.

# 44. Pocket Cabin Trail

Highlights: Spectacular views

Seasons: All year

Distance: 15.7 miles

Time: 6 hours

Difficulty Rating: Strenuous

High Elevation: 5,080 feet **Low Elevation:** 4,660 feet

USGS Topographic Maps: Diamond Point, McDonald Mountain, Payson South, Payson North

Connecting Rides: 43. Preacher Canyon, 46. Schoolhouse Canyon (if you take the Star Valley option)

Access: Take Arizona 260 east 7 miles. Look for the first turnoff to the right after Lion Springs Road. There is a sign marking the FS 436 road. Start and end here.

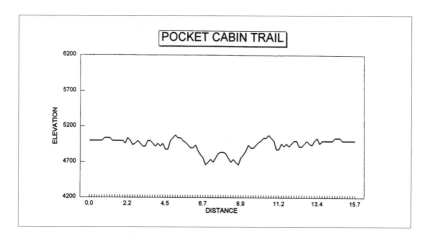

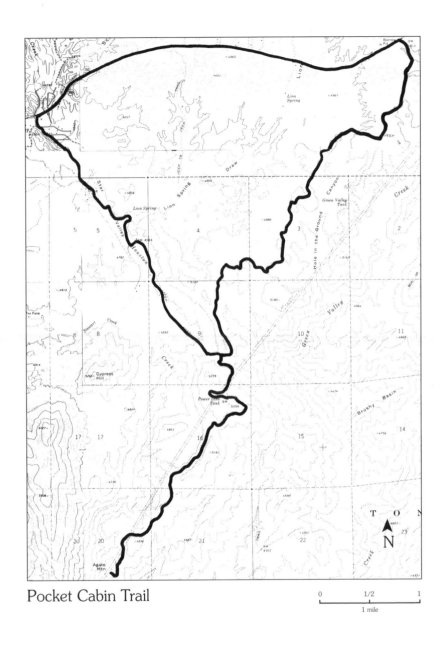

Pocket Cabin Trail

0   1/2   1

1 mile

The Route

Turn right off of FS 436 on to FS 371, just a few yards after the start of this ride. Take FS 371 up a small hill to a tank. Stick to the main road here and ignore all of the side roads, as this is a popular motorcycle playground. In fact, along this entire ride you will want to stick to the main road. It is maintained by the Arizona Public Service so they can service their powerlines.

Go up and down a ways until you come to a good intersection (1.2 miles). The road straight ahead dead-ends at a powerline tower. Turn right.

The road climbs up through piñon pines and juniper, and passes back and forth over the top of the ridge. When you are on the north side of the ridge the views to Diamond Point are good, and when you are on the south side you are looking into the aptly named Hole-in-the-Ground Canyon. Pass through a gate and then drop into one of the many drainages in the area. There is a turn to the left that looks good, but it dead-ends at the powerlines (3.1 miles). Keep going around to the right.

Drop into a saddle and look for the steep trail that leads down to the west and into Star Valley (4.4 miles). This makes a good turn-around point if you do not want to continue on.

Straight ahead is a disheartening "King Kong" ascent, steep and long. Unfortunately, you can see it all from here. Once you reach the top of this hill you will pass under the powerlines (4.9 miles) and by Powerline Tank (5.2 miles).

Ride out to the edge of the hill (5.5 miles). The trail to your left leads down to Pocket Cabin. The cabin is about 2.5 miles from here, beyond a couple of rocky, King Kong hills.

Your trail heads off to the right and more or less follows the ridge line to the left of the powerlines, and ends at an impressive cliff on top of Agate Mountain, about 800 feet above McDonald Creek (7.8 miles). Turn around here and head back to the low saddle on the other side of the hill and powerlines.

You can go back to your car the way you came, or you can be more adventurous. The adventurous route takes you to the west from this saddle—*straight down* into Star Valley. Actually, the road is straight down only for about the first 0.25 mile, then it levels out a bit and soon becomes undulating. In fact, you may start wishing for the straight down section again as the road repeatedly climbs and descends several short, steep hills.

This road ends at a ranch and a paved road. Turn right here and then turn right again at the stop sign. Follow the paved road about 1.5 miles through Star Valley and back out to Highway 260. Turn right on the highway and head back to your car, about 4 miles.

Notes

Andrew, Sam, and William Houston, cousins of the famous Sam Houston from Texas, purchased land in Star Valley in 1876. They brought in three hundred Durham cattle in 1878. Apparently, when they got back from the cattle drive, a man named John Starr was living in their cabin. The brothers named the valley after him.

History doesn't reveal what the brothers thought of Mr. Starr. He was eventually killed by Apache Indians at the ranch.

A school was opened in 1887, but it survived only a couple of years as trails to Payson were improved and students traveled there for school.

In 1895 an Italian immigrant named Louis Barnini settled in the lower part of the valley. He built the foundation and the fireplace of his cabin from surrounding prehistoric Native American ruins.

During the 1930s, Walter and Sarah Haught built a spring-fed reservoir in the valley and raised trout in the 56-degree water. Fish eggs were shipped in from two fish hatcheries, one in Boston and the other in Utah. The eggs were sent by train to Phoenix in the winter, when it was easier to keep them cool. Once they got to Phoenix they were packed in ice and trucked seven hours over the Apache Trail to Star Valley. The Haughts sold the fish for one dollar per pound to anyone willing to pay for the privilege of fishing in their pond.

45. Mayor's Cup

Highlights: Use every gear on your bike

Seasons: All year

Distance: 6.3 miles

Time: 1.5 hours

Difficulty Rating: Difficult

High Elevation: 5,000 feet   **Low Elevation:** 4,680 feet

USGS Topographic Maps: Diamond Point, Payson North

Connecting Rides: 23. Gilliland Gap, 46. Schoolhouse Canyon

Access: Head 4 miles east on Arizona 260, passing through Star Valley. Look for a dirt road to the left of the highway at the east end of Star Valley. It is past the car dealership but before the highway narrows. Turn left onto the dirt road (FS 433) and follow it for about 0.75 mile until it dead-ends at a gravel pit.

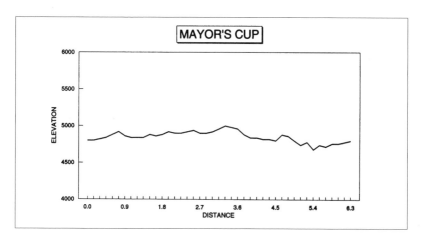

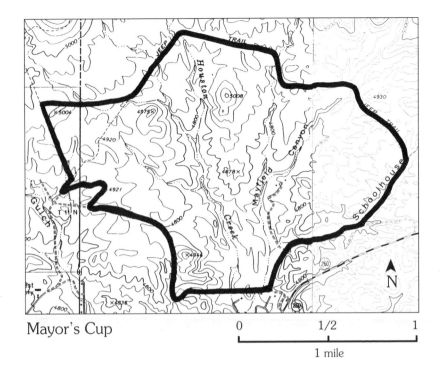

Mayor's Cup

0   1/2   1

1 mile

The Route

The trail starts just to the north of the gravel pit on the other side of the wash. Follow the trail to the east as it climbs up the wash. Turn left at the third little trail you see (0.4 mile).

There are a number of small hills and side trails here. Stick to the main trail as it rolls out toward Houston Mesa and then swings around to the left. The trail ends at a T-intersection (2.2 miles). The trail to the right leads up to Walnut Flats. You should turn left.

The road drops quickly into a wash. On the other side of the wash the jeep road climbs over the top of a hill, but take the single-track trail that leads to your right, just past the wash (2.7 miles). This trail gets a lot of use, so you shouldn't have any difficulty finding it.

The trail winds through the forest until it comes out on top of a hill. Head to the south down the steep hill to a fence (4.0 miles). Avoid the road through the gate to your right. Turn left and climb up the short, steep hill. At the top of this hill, take the trail to your right and descend past the old seismograph bunker to another T-intersection.

The road to the right is blocked by a fence. Take the road up to the left. Once you get to the top of this little hill, the trail you want twists down to the right and heads over a small saddle before it drops down to Houston Creek.

Both the left and the right trails you see from here will take you over the small hill straight ahead. Cross over the hill and drop back onto the road. Go left and return to your car.

Notes

This ride may sound complicated, but it is the site of the annual Payson Mayor's Cup Bike Race, so it gets a lot of use. Every spring, over five hundred mountain bike riders come to Payson to compete in this race. I list this ride as *difficult* (as opposed to *moderate*) because it is easy to take a wrong turn, and that may lead you to do more riding than you bargained for.

This area of Star Valley was homesteaded in the early 1900s by Anderson and Josephine Franklin of McKinney, Texas. They had been leasing land in the lower valley and decided to start their own ranch. Josephine's father, Rufus B. Brown, homesteaded acreage next to the Franklins. This ride circumnavigates their holdings.

46. Schoolhouse Canyon

Highlights: Views of Diamond Point

Seasons: All year, except after a snowstorm

Distance: 8.3 miles

Time: 3 hours

Difficulty Rating: Difficult

High Elevation: 5,360 feet   **Low Elevation:** 4,700 feet

USGS Topographic Maps: Diamond Point

Connecting Rides: 23. Gilliland Gap, 45. Mayor's Cup

Access: Head 4 miles east on Arizona 260, passing through Star Valley. Look for a dirt road to the left of the highway at the east end of Star Valley. It is past the car dealership but before the highway narrows. Turn left onto the dirt road (FS 433) and follow it for about 0.75 mile until it dead-ends at a gravel pit.

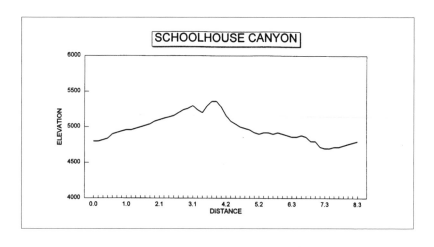

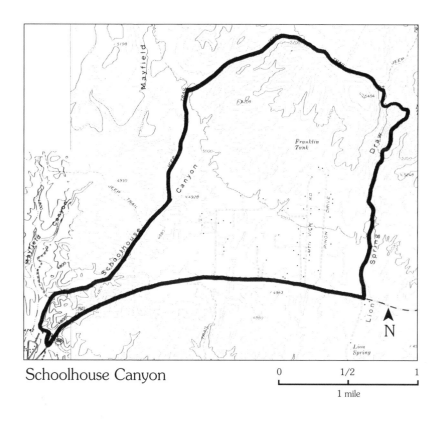

Schoolhouse Canyon

0   1/2   1

1 mile

The Route

The trail starts just to the north of the gravel pit on the other side of the wash. Follow the trail to the east as it climbs up the wash. Ignore the trails leading off to the left.

After a while the trail climbs away from the wash bottom and tops out on a short, steep hill. From here, the trail rolls a bit, trending downhill. Just after this "flat" section, a trail leads to the right (1.5 miles). This is the trail to Schoolhouse Canyon.

The trail dips in and out of the wash. At one point the trail forks, each direction looking correct. Take the right fork and ride up the wash.

46. Schoolhouse Canyon   **197**

At the saddle pass through a gate and follow the wash downhill. When the wash widens out a little, look for a very steep jeep trail to your left (3.4 miles). Push your bike up here and check out Neal Tank (3.6 miles). The views of Diamond Point are nice from here. Take the trail to the right as it climbs up the steep hill, then bomb down the other side.

The trail rejoins the wash, which you should follow downstream. Pass under the powerlines and then turn right at the highway (5.2 miles). Follow the highway back to the turn for the gravel pit (7.3 miles) and then follow that road back to your car.

TOP OF THE RIM

The crown of the Rim Country. The Mogollon Rim is actually the edge of the Colorado Plateau. The top is flat but cut by deep canyons that slope away to the north. Visitors are surprised when they see the canyons, as all of the paved roads stay along the flatter sections of the Rim. The routes in this section generally follow the ridges or the canyon bottoms, but occasionally they traverse the steep canyon sides.

The views here, whether from the edge of the Rim or from the edge of one of the many canyons, are spectacular. It is easy to see why this was among the favorite hiding places of American Indians during the late 1800s. In fact, it was not until General George Crook started a trail along the Rim from Prescott to Fort Apache in eastern Arizona that area tribes capitulated to white settlement.

The rocks here are nearly all sedimentary, and the routes are generally rocky with sections of dirt that can be muddy.

The vegetation is a mixture of pine, spruce, fir, and aspen trees. This is prime habitat for elk and black bear. With luck, you will see some elk, but consider yourself blessed if you see a bear; they generally shy away from people.

The Rim top is one of the most visited outdoor recreation areas in the state. Watch for vehicles close to the highway and along many back roads. Even when you feel as if you are miles from nowhere, you are likely to run into people. Fortunately, the Forest Service has set aside an area around Woods Canyon and Willow Springs Lakes that is closed to motorized vehicles, but open to mountain bikes. The many campgrounds make it a convenient area for an extended stay.

 # 47. Rim View

Highlights: General Crook Trail, views from the Rim

Seasons: Spring through fall

Distance: 4.8 miles

Time: 1.5 hours

Difficulty Rating: Easy

High Elevation: 7,640 feet   **Low Elevation:** 7,560 feet

USGS Topographic Maps: Woods Canyon

Connecting Rides: 48. Al Fulton Point, 50. Willow Springs Ridge

Access: Take Arizona 260 east about 30 miles until you are on top of the Rim. Turn left onto Rim Road. Park in the parking area on your right, just after turning in.

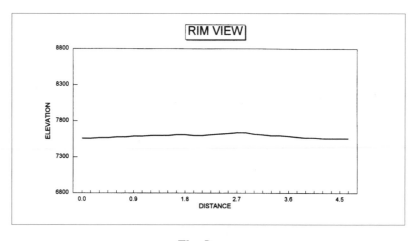

The Route

Follow the sign to General Crook Trail. This abandoned road rolls gently through woods and meadows until it comes out at the Woods

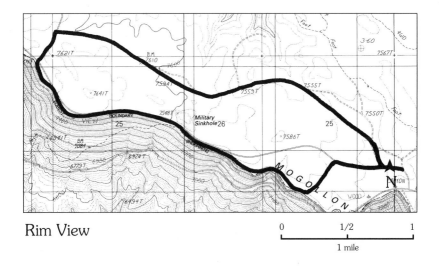

Rim View

0   1/2   1

1 mile

Canyon Lake entrance road (2.3 miles). Turn left on this paved road and follow it out to Rim Road (2.6 miles).

Cross the road and go into the viewpoint parking lot. There is a paved trail that tracks along the edge of the Rim. You can ride on it (to the left), but please be careful as this is a designated physically challenged recreation area.

At the end of this trail get back on the road for a few yards to get past the small canyon. Once you are past the canyon, go back out to the Rim edge and pick up the dirt trail. Be very careful along here. A crash could be disastrous. Follow this all the way down to a trail intersection. Turn left, away from the Rim, and head back to the Rim View Campground (4.2 miles). (The trail leading straight ahead quickly dies out.)

Notes

General George Crook was sent to Arizona in 1871. His assignment was to relocate Apaches to reservations. He was experienced in conflicts with American Indians, traveled light, and was well-respected by friends and foe. The military headquarters for Arizona was at Fort Whipple near Prescott, but the site of the most heated conflict was at

Some of the spectacular views from along the Rim's edge.

Top of the Rim

Fort Apache, in eastern Arizona. Travel between the forts was arduous and Crook felt that a more direct route was needed.

In August 1871, Crook led a small cavalry up onto the Rim near present-day Show Low and turned west along the Rim. It was not long before they realized they would have to stick to the edge of the Rim to avoid the deep, rugged canyons to the north. It was tough going, but they found water in the many small tanks and lakes along the way.

They finally turned north away from the edge of the Rim at General Springs and went north to Stoneman Lake Road so they could get to Prescott more quickly.

Work on the trail began in 1872. Crook planned to use the trail to keep Fort Apache supplied and also to be above the Apache, who liked to spend summers in the Rim Country and use it as a sanctuary. By 1873 supplies were being moved by pack train over the trail, and in September 1874 the first wagon train crossed it. The first woman to cross the trail, Martha Summerhayes, was on this train. She later wrote about her rough experiences in her book *Vanished Arizona: Recollections of the Army Life of a New England Woman*.

The Atlantic and Pacific Railroad reached Holbrook in 1879. Fort Apache could then be supplied more directly from there. Use of the trail diminished, but the army continued to patrol it until 1893. The Rim Road was built in 1928, and follows the original trail in many places.

48. Al Fulton Point

Highlights: Rim Lakes Visitor Center

Seasons: Spring through fall

Distance: 10 miles

Time: 2 hours

Difficulty Rating: Easy

High Elevation: 7,650 feet   **Low Elevation:** 7,460 feet

USGS Topographic Maps: Woods Canyon, OW Point

Connecting Rides: 47. Rim View

Access: Head east on Arizona 260 about 30 miles until you are on top of the Rim. Park at the visitor center to the right just after getting to the top.

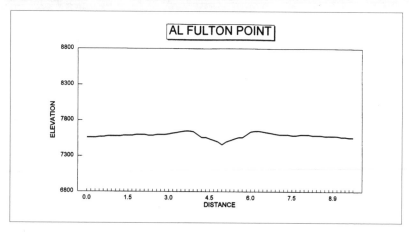

The Route

Leave from the visitor center and travel east on the dirt road. This is a dispersed camping area. Turn left at Young Road, a veritable dirt superhighway (2 miles). Turn right at the next dirt road, marked FS 181 (2.4 miles).

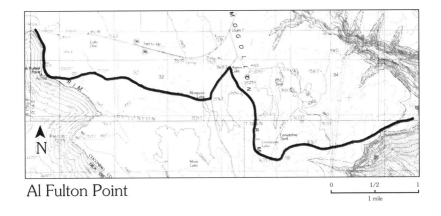

Al Fulton Point

0   1/2   1
⊢━━━━━━━━━━━━━━━┥
          1 mile

Follow this road uphill to the powerlines, then downhill to where the road ends at the top of a canyon (5 miles). Turn around here and follow the same route back.

Notes

Al Fulton was a shepherd for Jack Woods (see notes section of Lake Overlook, page 234). Fulton may have been ambushed and killed by someone in the cattle faction during the Pleasant Valley War of the 1880s.

49. Rim Line to OW Point

Highlights: OW Point

Seasons: Spring through fall

Distance: 7.3 miles

Time: 2 hours

Difficulty Rating: Moderate

High Elevation: 7,700 feet   **Low Elevation:** 7,540 feet

USGS Topographic Maps: Woods Canyon, OW Point

Access: Follow Arizona 260 east 32 miles over the top of the Rim. Turn right at the Young Road turnoff 2 miles after the visitor center. Look for the second decent dirt road on your right, about 1.5 miles after you turn onto Young Road.

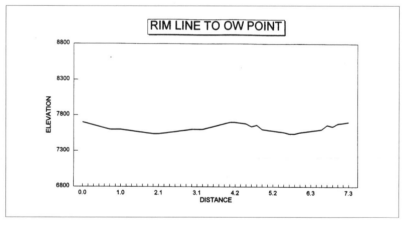

The Route

Take this road west until it ends in a meadow. The views are not especially good even though you are close to the edge of the Rim. Turn around at the dead-end (1.9 miles).

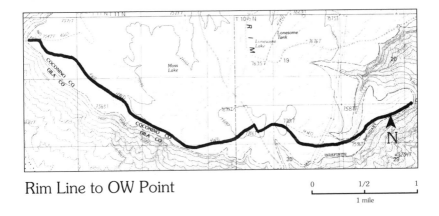

Rim Line to OW Point

Head back to Young Road and cross it (4 miles). This smooth road (FS 79) leads to OW Point (5.7 miles) and some fantastic views. Turn around at the dead-end.

Notes

OW Point is named after OW Ranch, visible in the valley below the point. OW Ranch was a stopover for cattle drives on the Crooked Trail to Holbrook (see notes section of Gentry Giant Loop, pages 228–229).

50. Willow Springs Ridge

Highlights: Chevelon Canyon views, flat ride

Seasons: Spring through fall

Distance: 10.4 miles

Time: 2 hours

Difficulty Rating: Very easy

High Elevation: 7,555 feet   **Low Elevation:** 7,565 feet

USGS Topographic Maps: Woods Canyon

Connecting Rides: 47. Rim View

Access: Take Arizona 260 east about 30 miles until you are on top of the Rim. Turn left onto Rim Road. Park in the parking area on your right, just after turning in.

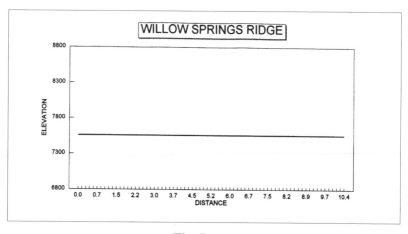

The Route

Ride past the gate and look for the bike trail (FS 235) signs. This is a designated mountain bike trail, so there are signs to follow. No motor vehicles are allowed. Head out to the edge of Chevelon Canyon and back.

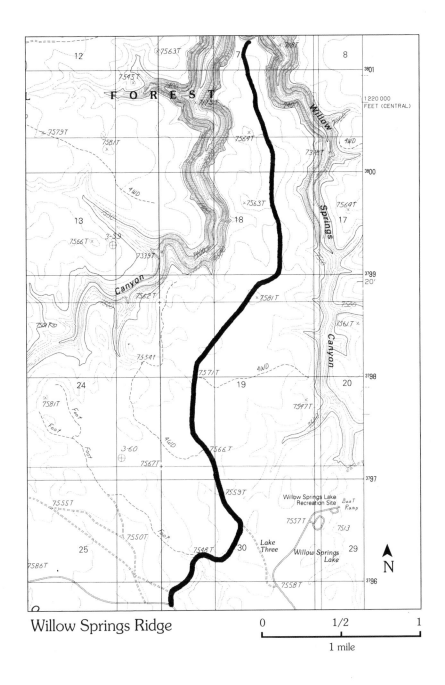

12	7563T	7	8

F O R E S T

7545T

7579T

7581T

7564T

7343T

Willow

13

7566T

3-59

7339T

Canyon

7562T

18

7563T

7581T

7561T

Springs

7564T

17

Canyon

7504 Rd

7554T

7571T

4WD

19

7547T

20

24

7581T

Foot

Foot

Foot

4WD

3-60

7567T

7566T

7559T

Willow Springs Lake
Recreation Site

Boat
Ramp

7557T

7513

7555T

25

7550T

Foot

7548T

30

Lake
Three

Willow Springs
Lake

29

7586T

7558T

N

Willow Springs Ridge

0   1/2   1

1 mile

Notes

Chevelon Canyon was formed by Chevelon Creek. When Lt. Lorenzo Sitgreaves first came through here in 1851, in his reconnaissance of Arizona, he named the creek Big Dry Creek and the canyon Big Dry Wash. Gradually the name of the creek and canyon changed to Chevelon for a trapper who accidentally poisoned himself by eating wild parsnips. Mr. Chevelon is buried in the northern reaches of the canyon.

 **51. Horse Trap Lake**

Highlights: Willow Springs Lake

Seasons: Spring through fall

Distance: 13 miles

Time: 3 hours

Difficulty Rating: Moderate

High Elevation: 7,660 feet   **Low Elevation:** 7,460 feet

USGS Topographic Maps: Woods Canyon, OW Point, Porcupine Ridge

Connecting Rides: 52. Larson Ridge

Access: Follow Arizona 260 east about 35 miles, across the edge of the Rim, to the Canyon Point Campground. Across from the campground entrance, on the left side of the road, is FS road 237. Turn in there. Park in the parking area at the first road to your left.

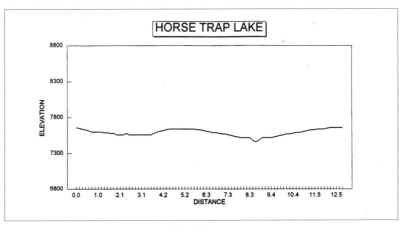

The Route

This ride follows a designated mountain bike trail. Go straight at the small powerlines (0.1 mile) instead of turning right. Turn right at

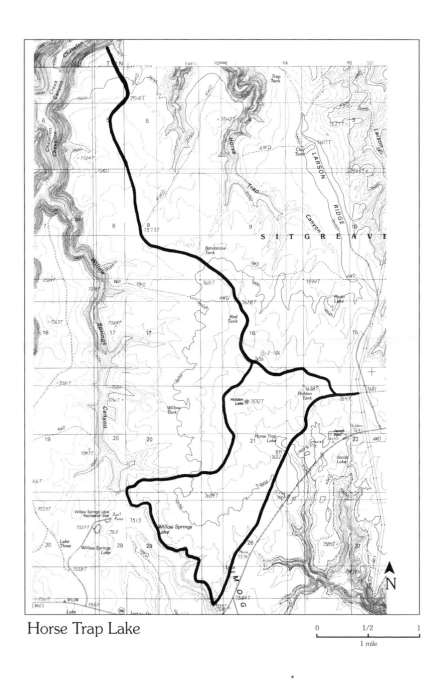

Horse Trap Lake

```
0          1/2          1
├─────────┼─────────┤
        1 mile
```

On the road, near Willow Springs Lake.

the T-intersection (2.1 miles) and pass Willow Springs Lake on the rocky road. Follow the bike icon signs through this section and take the next right (3.3 miles). Ride up the small hill past the water-filled borrow pits. When you get to the good road (FS 236, 5.4 miles) turn left to reach a stunning vista of Chevelon Canyon (8.6 miles) on a fairly flat road. This road is not marked with bike icons.

Turn around at the dead-end and follow the road back. Go straight at the intersection with the road from the borrow pit and follow the bike icon signs back to your car.

Notes

This was the first designated mountain bike trail in the Rim Country.

52. Larson Ridge

Highlights: Chevelon and Larson Canyons
Seasons: Spring through fall
Distance: 18.5 miles
Time: 5 hours
Difficulty Rating: Difficult
High Elevation: 7,680 feet   **Low Elevation:** 7,200 feet
USGS Topographic Maps: OW Point, Weimer Point
Connecting Rides: 51. Horse Trap Lake
Access: Follow Arizona 260 east about 35 miles, across the edge of the Rim, to the Canyon Point Campground. Across from the campground entrance, on the left side of the road, is FS road 247. Turn in there. Park in the parking area at the first road to your left.

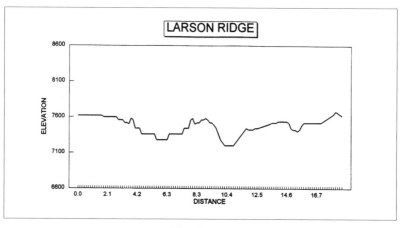

The Route

Start on the road that is *not* blocked by a gate, underneath the powerlines. The road drifts away from the powerlines and angles

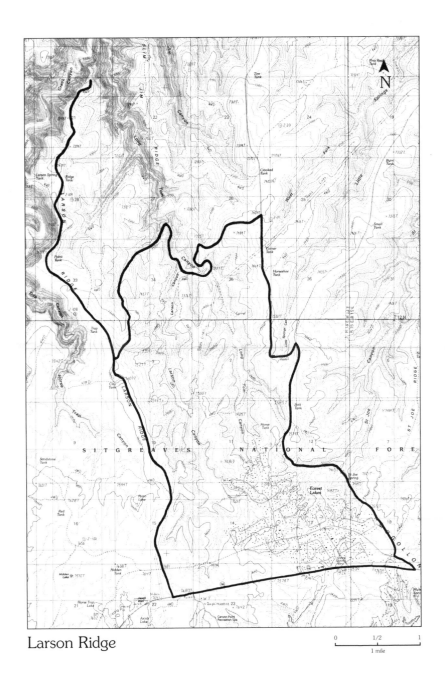

Larson Ridge

0   1/2   1
1 mile

downward, offering great views of Chevelon Canyon to your left. Take note of FS 172 on your right as you ride out to the viewpoint (2.8 miles)—you will take this road on your way back. The road becomes rougher as it gets close to the point. There are several roads out here that lead to nice views along the edge. Turn around at the dead-end (5.8 miles).

Go back to FS 172 and turn left down into the canyon (8.8 miles). This descent is very steep and rocky but without any sharp turns, so you can really pick up some speed.

The road follows the canyon bottom past a meadow and rock outcropping (10.4 miles) and then climbs out the other side. When the road turns you will get a good view of the canyon.

Turn right on the wide FS 170 dirt road (12.1 miles) and pass under the powerlines. Turn right again at FS 99 (13.6 miles). Go left at the sign to Forest Lakes (14.5 miles) and follow this road out to the highway (16.2 miles). Turn right on the highway and follow it back to your car.

Notes

Larson Ridge and Larson Canyon are probably named after a Mormon who settled here in the 1880s. The first settlers arrived in the 1870s and were cattlemen. We don't know much more about these people. During the 1850s and 1860s, Mormons went to great efforts to proselytize Scandinavians. Larson was probably a Scandinavian Mormon sent here to colonize for the church.

St. Joe Ridge was along a trail to Joseph City, named St. Joseph on early maps.

53. Canyon Point View and 54. Late Night Ski Trail

Highlights: Forest cruising, canyon views

Seasons: Spring through fall

Distance: 4 miles each

Time: 1 hour each

Difficulty Rating: 53—very easy, 54—easy

High Elevation: 7,640 feet **Low Elevation:** 7,440 feet

USGS Topographic Maps: OW Point

Connecting Rides: 55. Feeling Blue on Wedding Day

Access: Take Arizona 260 east about 35 miles, across the top of the Rim, to the Canyon Point Campground. Across from the campground entrance, on the left side of the road, is FS road 237. Turn in there and park in the parking area at the first road to your left.

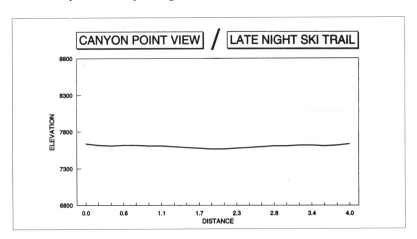

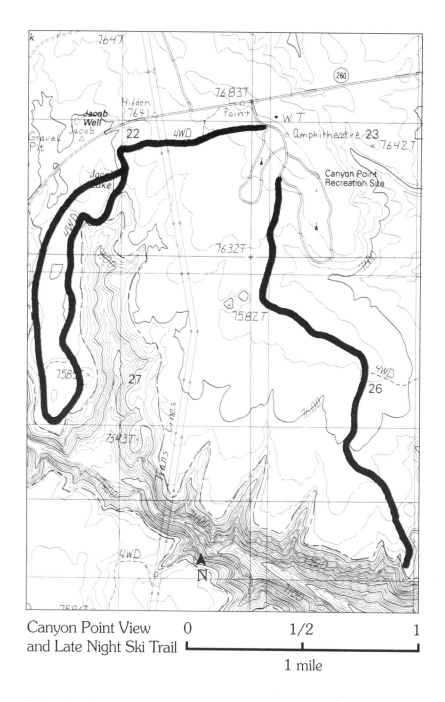

Canyon Point View
and Late Night Ski Trail

0   1/2   1

1 mile

The Routes

The Canyon Point View ride begins just after you get into the campground "B" loop on the right. Follow the blue trail markers. The ski-touring center calls this the Back Alley.

The Late Night Ski Trail starts just to the right of the ticket booth at the campground. Follow the red trail markers.

Notes

Canyon Point Campground was built in the early 1960s and renovated in 1993.

55. Feeling Blue on Wedding Day and 56. Sheep Springs Point

Highlights: Forest cruising, canyon views

Seasons: Spring through fall

Distance: 55—4.5 miles, 56—6.2 miles

Time: 1 to 2 hours each

Difficulty Rating: 55—easy, 56—very easy

High Elevation: 7,640 feet   **Low Elevation:** 7,440 feet

USGS Topographic Maps: OW Point

Access: Take Arizona 260 east about 36 miles until you reach Forest Lakes, about 5 miles past the visitor center. Stop at the ski lodge on the right side of the highway.

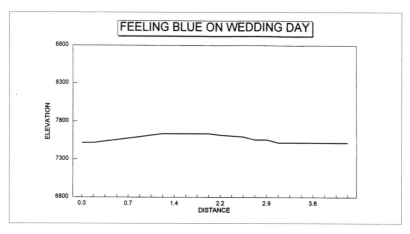

The Routes

Pick up the trail for Feeling Blue on Wedding Day just to the left of the ski lodge. This ride is a loop made of two connecting ski trails.

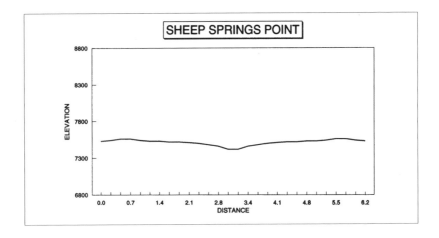

You can follow either the white or the blue trail markers for this forest loop.

Sheep Springs Point is called Rim Run by skiers. It begins to the east of the General Store on an old logging road. Follow the orange trail markers out to the viewpoint.

Notes

They will be happy to give you one of the ski-touring maps for these rides at the ski lodge. The lodge was built in the early 1980s and services hundreds of cross-country skiers every winter.

Forest Lakes began as a series of manganese mining claims taken out by John Patrick of Heber, Arizona, in 1958. Some work was done on the claims at that time. The claims were patented by Mr. Patrick, who subdivided and sold the land. The Arizona Department of Mines and Minerals' chief engineer reported on the property in 1987. He found that the mine prospects were being used as a sanitary landfill. An assay of the ore did reveal manganese in an economically viable amount.

Top of the Rim

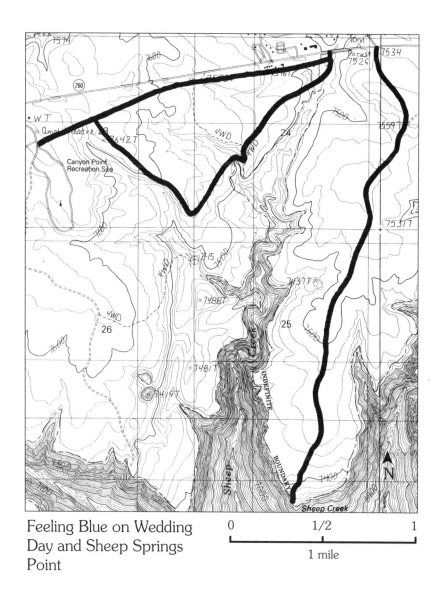

Feeling Blue on Wedding
Day and Sheep Springs
Point

0   1/2   1

1 mile

The ski lodge at Forest Lakes.

57. Gentry Giant Loop

Highlights: Black Canyon Lake, Gentry Fire Tower
Seasons: Spring through fall
Distance: 14.3 miles
Time: 4 hours
Difficulty Rating: Difficult
High Elevation: 7,720 feet   **Low Elevation:** 6,880 feet
USGS Topographic Maps: Brookbank Point
Connecting Rides: 58. Bull Flat Ridge
Access: Follow Arizona 260 east about 39.5 miles until you come to the FS 300 road on your right. Follow this dirt road for about 5 miles to the Black Canyon Lake Campground.

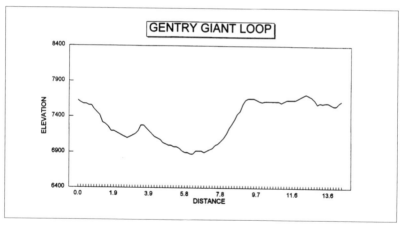

The Route

Follow the signed road down the canyon from the campground toward Black Canyon Lake. It follows along the ridge top and then drops down into the canyon. The vegetation is lush here. You can visit

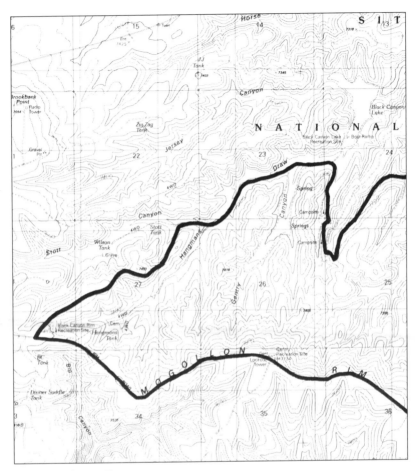

Gentry Giant Loop

the lake by turning left at the entrance road (2.8 miles). Please note that bikes are not allowed on the loop trail around the lake.

The ride continues straight ahead (or to the left if you are leaving the lake) over a hill. Look for the Baca family cemetery on the right in a stand of aspen trees (4.8 miles). As you get lower in the canyon you will see the fences belonging to BC Ranch. The road is paved in the ranch headquarters area to keep the dust down from passing vehicles.

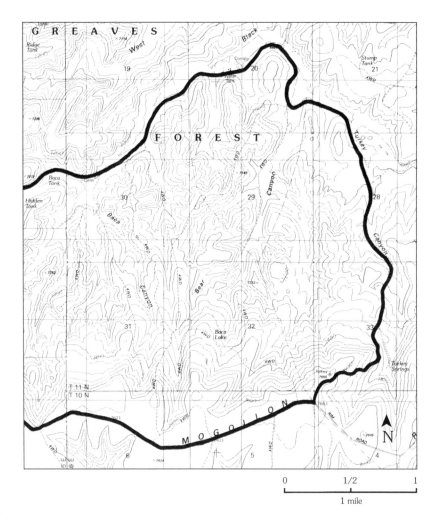

At the intersection by the ranch (6.1 miles), turn right and begin climbing back up to the Rim. There are a couple of ups and downs, but then the road begins to climb steadily and becomes increasingly steep until you get to the top of the Rim and FS 300 (9.2 miles). Turn right here.

This section is fairly flat and there are a number of old logging roads to the south as you ride along. All of these are great for exploring. They are not too steep and most come to an end out toward the Apache reservation.

Continue to follow the road along the Rim as it slopes up toward Gentry Lookout (12.4 miles). The views from the top of this spacious tower are great and it is well worth the climb if it is manned. Please do not enter the tower if there is no one there.

Follow the road downhill from the lookout and then uphill until you get back to the campground.

Notes

This ride is located along one of Arizona's main cattle trails, the Crooked Trail to Holbrook. Holbrook became an important cattle shipping center when the Atlantic and Pacific Railroad arrived there in 1879. Ranchers from all over the Rim Country would drive their cattle to Young in the Pleasant Valley. From there, they would drive the cattle toward the Rim, making two overnight stops along the way. Cattle were driven over the Rim in the area between the Gentry Lookout and the Black Canyon Campground. From there, they were driven down the Black Canyon, through where Black Canyon Lake is now, on into Heber, then finally to Holbrook. The cattle drive would take one week, if all went well. The trail was used steadily over the years until, in the early 1900s, ranchers began to depend on trucks to get their cattle to market. It is estimated that during the life of the trail as many as a quarter of a million cattle may have been driven across it. By the 1930s, the Crooked Trail was gone.

Near the present-day entrance to the lake, holding pens were built for the drives by Old Man Gentry, a local pioneer. The lake was opened to fishing in 1963.

The Baca family had a ranch where the small cemetery now stands. Juan and Damasia Baca lived in New Mexico before moving to Holbrook, where they opened a cafe. When their business burned down they decided to take up ranching. Most of the ranches in this area ran sheep and the Bacas were no different. The family moved here and Juan began building a cabin that took him twelve years to finish. Many of the Baca children were female and their ranch became a popular hangout for young men at a place and time when few young women lived in the area.

Juan Baca was buried in the cemetery in 1903. After Juan died, Damasia continued to run the ranch with her children and their families.

The youngest Baca daughter, Dora, died in 1916 and was buried next to her father. She had been invited to a dance in Chandler. She washed her long, thick hair before she went. Unfortunately, the car she rode in did not have a top and Dora got chilled on the way to the dance. By the time she returned she had pneumonia and died a couple of days later. Damasia died in 1934.

The BC Ranch on the turn to Holbrook was established in 1886. J. D. Houck and his wife, Beatrice, lived in Holbrook and moved to the ranch to raise sheep. At this time, the feud between the Grahams and the Tewksburys, known as the Pleasant Valley War, was raging. Houck took up with the Grahams on the "sheep side" of the war and is reputed to have been one of the most bloodthirsty killers in the history of the state. In 1887 he became a deputy sheriff. Using this as a front, he killed or helped kill at least six men. His younger brother thought that he may have killed as many as sixty men, not counting American Indians. People were so afraid of Houck that nobody crossed him. He lived a long but unhappy life.

Near Black Canyon Campground are the graves of three young men who were among Houck's victims in the Pleasant Valley War. In a somewhat convoluted tale, the three were accused of stealing. They worked as cattle ranchers but had no interest in the war. One morning Houck and a posse of men arrived at the young men's ranch. They called them out and tied them up. Houck claimed to have a warrant for their arrest, but that he forgot to bring it with him.

The posse tied nooses around the necks of two of them. At first the posse had only wanted to scare them, but things got out of hand. They threw the ropes over a tree limb and hanged the two men while their companion, Jamie Stott, was forced to watch. They then hanged Stott.

The posse left the bodies hanging as a message. It was three days before anyone got up the courage to cut the bodies down and bury them.

Years later, a story circulated about a gold ring that had been buried with Jamie. Before coming to Arizona, Jamie lived in Massachusetts where his father worked in a cloth mill. His father lost both of his arms when he tried to save a worker from one of the machines at the factory. His wedding band was recovered and the older Stott gave the ring to his young son before Jamie set out to Arizona.

In the 1940s, Fred Turly, a local dude ranch owner, his foreman, and some guests dug up the bodies of the three unfortunate young men. Sure enough, there was the ring. The foreman came back later, took the ring from the grave, and gave it to his new bride.

58. Bull Flat Ridge

Highlights: Twin Lakes

Seasons: Spring through fall

Distance: 4.6 miles

Time: 1.5 hours

Difficulty Rating: Easy

High Elevation: 7,724 feet   **Low Elevation:** 7,460 feet

USGS Topographic Maps: Brookbank Point

Connecting Rides: 57. Gentry Giant Loop

Access: Follow Arizona 260 east about 39.5 miles until you come to FS 300 on your right. Follow this dirt road for about 7 miles to Gentry Lookout.

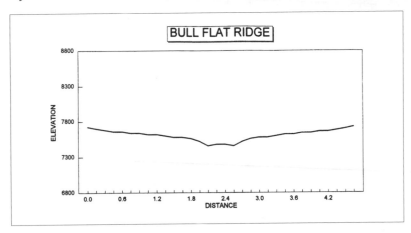

The Route

This route starts directly opposite the Gentry picnic ground, south of FS 300. Follow the main road out the ridge. This area was heavily

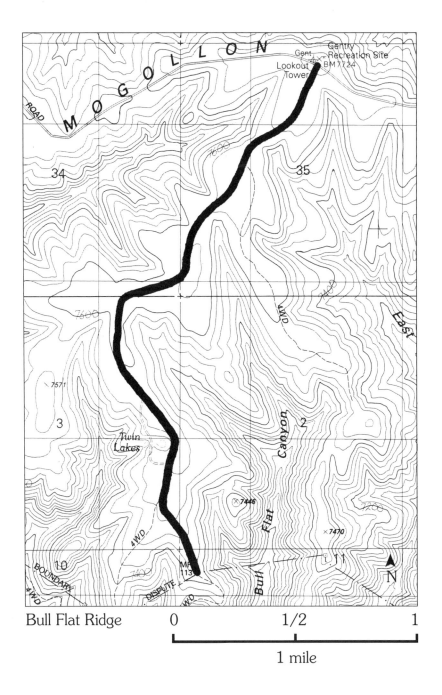

MOGOLLON

Gentry
Lookout
Tower
Gentry
Recreation Site
BM 7724

34

35

7600

7600

4WD

7600

7571

East
Canyon

3

Twin
Lakes

2

×7446

Flat

×7470

4WD

7400

10

BOUNDARY

4WD

MR
113

DISPUTE

4WD

Bull

11

N

Bull Flat Ridge   0   1/2   1

1 mile

logged not too many years ago, so it is very open. As you go down the hill you will notice a stand of old-growth pines off to your right. This is the area of the tiny Twin Lakes (1.6 miles). The road ends a little farther down the ridge (2.3 miles). Turn around here.

Notes

This is a good ride to see the difference between a logged and an unlogged forest.

59. Lake Overlook

Highlights: View of Woods Canyon Lake

Seasons: Spring through fall

Distance: 1.6 miles

Time: Minutes

Difficulty Rating: Very easy

High Elevation: 7,660 feet   **Low Elevation:** 7,620 feet

USGS Topographic Maps: Woods Canyon

Connecting Rides: 60. North Woods Canyon, 61. Palomino Lake, 62. Oak Groves, 63. Promontory Butte

Access: Travel east on Arizona 260 for 30 miles to the top of the Rim. Turn left at Rim Road. Follow this road until it turns to dirt. Do not turn down the Woods Canyon Lake entrance road. Look for FS 195 on the right, 2 miles past the start of the dirt. Pull in here and park at the end of the road by the gate.

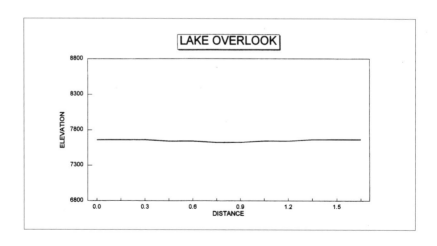

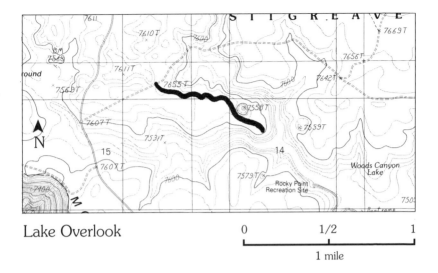

Lake Overlook

0   1/2   1

1 mile

The Route

Look for a dirt road leading from campsite 54 or 57 on the south side of FS 195. Turn onto this old logging road and follow it to the east to the end of the ridge. You can see Woods Canyon Lake from here. Return the same way.

Notes

Woods Canyon is named after Jack Woods, a sheep rancher here in the 1880s. Jack was quite an entrepreneur who arrived in Winslow with the railroad in 1879. He built a butcher shop, boardinghouse, and store (the first brick building) in Winslow. He controlled a far-flung ranching empire. The property in the canyon was managed by Al Fulton (see notes section to Al Fulton Point, page 205).

The lake was built between 1956 and 1958 by the Arizona Game and Fish Department and cost $69,000. It was revamped in 1965. Woods Canyon Lake has become the center of outdoor recreation for people in Arizona. It is so heavily used that the Forest Service has had to create a number of restrictions. They designated dispersed camping areas, like FS 195, and, lucky for us, they created a huge non-motorized recreation area around the lake.

60. North Woods Canyon

Highlights: Pleasant ride through the forest

Seasons: Spring through fall

Distance: 8.5 miles

Time: 2 hours

Difficulty Rating: Moderate

High Elevation: 7,660 feet   **Low Elevation:** 7,520 feet

USGS Topographic Maps: Woods Canyon

Connecting Rides: 59. Lake Overlook, 61. Palomino Lake, 62. Oak Groves, 63. Promontory Butte

Access: Travel east on Arizona 260 for 30 miles to the top of the Rim. Turn left at Rim Road. Follow this road until it turns to dirt. Do not turn down the lake road. Look for the FS 195 road on the right two miles past the start of the dirt. Pull in here and park at the end of the road by the gate.

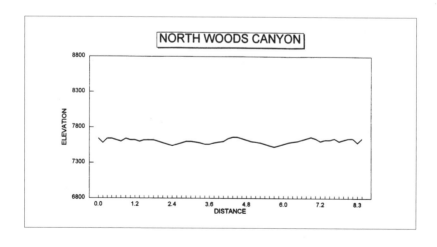

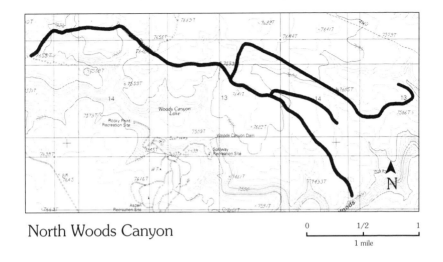

North Woods Canyon

0   1/2   1

1 mile

The Route

Ride under the gate and cross the wash. Head over the hill into the next smaller wash. Just out of this wash is a Y-intersection (0.9 mile). Stay to the right here and follow the road through this flat, open country. All the rest of the roads dead-end after this, so you won't need to worry about getting lost.

There is another intersection at 1.3 miles. Turn right and ride until you come to another intersection (1.8 miles). The road to the right dead-ends in the woods after about 1 mile. The road to the left dead-ends at a small natural lake after about 1 mile. Once you have finished exploring these roads go back to the last intersection and go north.

This road climbs a hill, then descends down toward the canyon, becoming rougher at the end. Turn around there and head all the way back to your car.

You can take any side trail you want on this ride without fear of getting lost. Except for the Y-intersection at the start of the ride, all the roads dead-end, so you can backtrack to get to where you need to be.

61. Palomino Lake

Highlights: Palomino Lake

Seasons: Spring through fall

Distance: 8.0 miles

Time: 2 hours

Difficulty Rating: Moderate

High Elevation: 7,680 feet   **Low Elevation:** 7,540 feet

USGS Topographic Maps: Woods Canyon

Connecting Rides: 59. Lake Overlook, 60. North Woods Canyon, 62. Oak Groves, 63. Promontory Butte

Access: Travel east on Arizona 260 for 30 miles to the top of the Rim. Turn left at Rim Road. Follow this road until it turns to dirt. Do not turn down the lake road. Look for the FS 195 road on the right 2 miles past the start of the dirt. Pull in here and park at the end of the road by the gate.

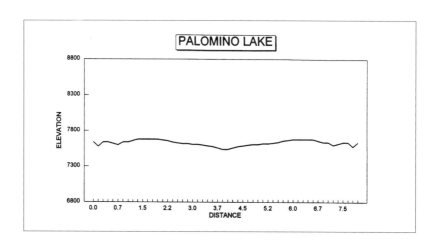

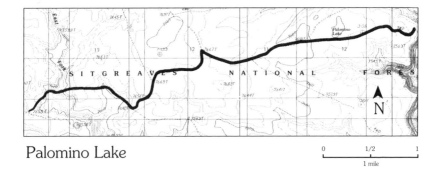

Palomino Lake

0   1/2   1
|————————|————————|
        1 mile

The Route

Ride under the gate and cross the wash. Head over the hill into the next smaller wash. Just out of this wash you will come to a Y-intersection (0.9 mile). Go left here. Ignore the faint, old road to the left as the road bends to the right. Just keep following the easiest-to-follow road. When you get to a T-intersection (2.1 miles), turn right.

There are dozens of old, flat logging roads here. They are great for exploring, but it is easy to get turned around. Don't get lost. Follow the main road through here until you see Palomino Lake on your left (3.3 miles). This road dies out in the woods a little ways beyond here. Return by the same route.

62. Oak Groves

Highlights: Parklike setting with huge oak trees

Seasons: Spring through fall

Distance: 8.2 miles

Time: 2 hours

Difficulty Rating: Moderate

High Elevation: 7,740 feet   **Low Elevation:** 7,580 feet

USGS Topographic Maps: Woods Canyon, Porcupine Ridge

Connecting Rides: 59. Lake Overlook, 60. North Woods Canyon, 61. Palomino Lake

Access: Travel east on Arizona 260 for 30 miles to the top of the Rim. Turn left at Rim Road. Follow this road until it turns to dirt. Do not turn down the lake road. Look for the FS 195 road on the right 2 miles past the start of the dirt. Pull in here and park at the end of the road by the gate.

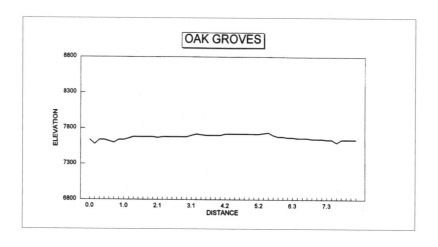

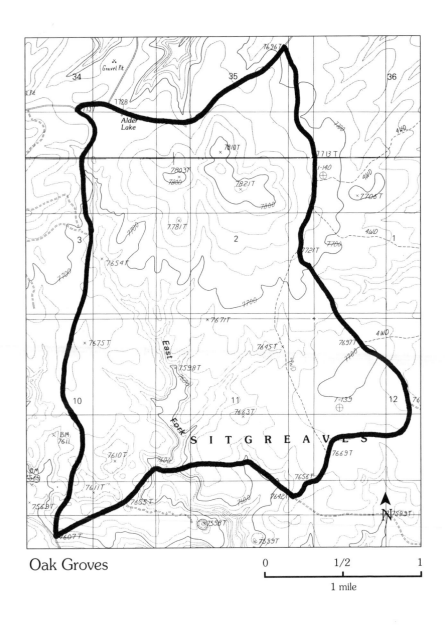

Oak Groves

0   1/2   1

1 mile

The Route

Ride under the gate and cross the wash. Head over the hill into the next smaller wash. Just out of this wash you will come to a Y-intersection (0.9 mile). Go left here. Ignore the faint, old road to the left as the road bends to the right. Just keep following the easiest-to-follow road. When you get to a T-intersection (2.1 miles), turn left. The oak groves are here.

The road gets rough through here as you pass a couple of dirt roads. At the next T-intersection (3.0 miles), go right and continue straight through the next intersection (3.3 miles). You will come out on FS 169 at Deer Lake (4.0 miles). Turn left here, then turn left at FS 300 (5.2 miles). Turn left once again at FS 195 (7.6 miles).

63. Promontory Butte

Highlights: Spectacular views

Seasons: Spring through fall

Distance: 10.4 miles

Time: 2.5 hours

Difficulty Rating: Moderate

High Elevation: 7,900 feet   **Low Elevation:** 7,680 feet

USGS Topographic Maps: Promontory Butte

Access: Travel east on Arizona 260 for 30 miles to the top of the Rim. Turn left at Rim Road. Follow this road (FS 300) until it turns to dirt and continue for another 9 miles. Follow the signs for Bear Canyon Lake. Turn left on FS 76 after you pass by the Promontory fire lookout tower. It is the road just before the turnoff to Bear Canyon Lake.

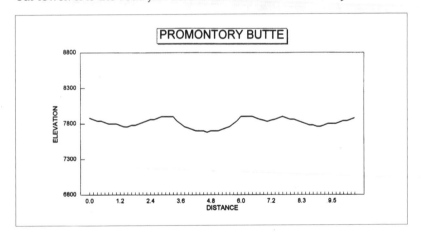

The Route

Follow FS 76 all the way down to the southeast corner of the butte (4.6 miles). The road gets rough toward the end, but the views

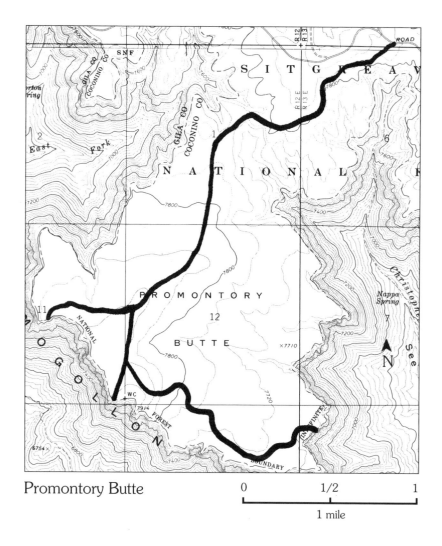

Promontory Butte

0   1/2   1

1 mile

are well worth it. Turn around and ride back up to the road marked FS 76B (6.4 miles). Turn left here and follow the road up the hill.

Near the top of the hill is a junction. Take the road to the right first. It will lead you past a small meadow and out to the edge of the butte after a little more than 0.5 mile. Turn around and go back to the junction. Turn right here and go uphill. The spectacular view is just over the top of the hill. The road slopes down to the point and

The Rim, as seen from Promontory Butte.

more or less dies out. Some old maps show a trail leading off the Rim here, but I can't imagine taking it. When you have had enough of the view, turn around and head back to your car.

Appendix A
For More Information About
Biking the Rim Country

Chevlon Ranger District, Forest Service
HC 62, Box 600, Winslow, Arizona 86047
(520) 289-2471
Maps, books, and forest information on "Top of the Rim" rides.

Forest Lakes Touring Center and Cabins
PO Box 1887, Forest Lakes, Arizona 85931
(520) 535-4047
Cabins open year-round. Cyclists are encouraged to use ski trails during the off-season. Trail maps are available at the lodge.

Heber Ranger District, Forest Service
PO Box 968, Overgaard, Arizona 85933
(520) 535-4481
Maps, books, and forest information for "Top of the Rim" rides.

Manzanita Cyclery
John and Simone Lake
107 South Beeline Highway, Payson, Arizona 85541
(in the IGA shopping center behind Pizza Hut)
(520) 474-0744
The best bike shop in the Rim Country. Current trail information as well as information about cycling events in the area.

Northern Gila County Historical Society Museum of the Forest
1001 West Main Street, Payson, Arizona 85541
(520) 474-3483
Displays pioneer memorabilia and a miniature model of an early sawmill. Genealogy and archeology libraries.

Payson Chamber of Commerce
PO Box 1380, Payson, Arizona 85547
1-800-672-9766 or (520) 474-4515
Information about where to stay, where to eat, and other local attractions.

Payson Ranger District, Forest Service
1009 East Highway 260, Payson, Arizona 85541
(520) 474-7900
Maps, books, and forest information for all areas described in this book *except* for the top of the Rim.

Tonto Creek Fish Hatchery
HC Route #2, Box 96-I, Payson, Arizona 85541
(520) 478-4220
State-of-the-art trout farm that supplies fish for dozens of lakes and streams in central Arizona.

Wide World of Maps
2626 West Indian School Road, Phoenix, Arizona 85017, and
1334 South Country Club Drive, Mesa, Arizona 85202
1-800-279-2350 or (602) 279-2323
Fax (602) 279-2350
Every map and book you can imagine on Arizona and the outdoors.

Zane Grey Museum
408 West Main Street #8, Payson, Arizona 85541
(520) 474-6243
Zane Grey memorabilia that was not destroyed in the Dude Fire.

Appendix B
Rides Grouped by Difficulty

VERY EASY RIDES
15. Sycamore Canyon
31. Logging Country
50. Willow Springs Ridge
53. Canyon Point View
56. Sheep Springs Point
59. Lake Overlook

EASY RIDES
19. Edge of Mesa Del
20. Walnut Flats
27. Whispering Pines
29. South Tonto Village
36. Campsite
37. Little Green Valley
47. Rim View
48. Al Fulton Point
54. Late Night Ski Trail
55. Feeling Blue on Wedding Day
58. Bull Flat Ridge

MODERATE RIDES
1. Stewart Pocket
2. Peach Orchard Springs
4. Round Valley
5. Oxbow Estates
8. Marysville Hill
12. Royal Flush
14. Ash Creek Canyon
16. Flowing Springs
24. The Crossings
25. Control Road West
28. Control Road East
30. Tonto Village Forest Loop
34. Diamond Point
35. Pyeatt Draw
42. Two-Sixty Trailhead
43. Preacher Canyon
49. Rim Line to OW Point
51. Horse Trap Lake
60. North Woods Canyon
61. Palomino Lake
62. Oak Groves
63. Promontory Butte

DIFFICULT RIDES
3. Snowstorm Mountain
9. Oxbow Hill
10. Wild Rye Creek
13. Gisela
17. Pine Canyon Overlook
18. Crackerjack
21. Shoofly and the River
22. Over the Diamond Rim
26. Washington Park
32. Roberts Draw
33. Mead Ranch
38. Bear Flats
39. Tonto Creek

DIFFICULT RIDES (cont.)
40. Horton Springs
41. Christopher Mountain
45. Mayor's Cup
46. Schoolhouse Canyon
52. Larson Ridge
57. Gentry Giant Loop

STRENUOUS
6. Cypress Thicket
7. Doll Baby Ranch
11. Table Mountain
23. Gilliland Gap
44. Pocket Cabin Trail

Bibliography and Suggested Reading

Abbey, Edward. *The Monkey Wrench Gang*. New York: Avon Books, 1975. This well-written novel does not touch on the Rim Country geographically, but it does in spirit. It spawned the *Earth First!* eco-terrorism movement. While I do not condone the methodology of the characters, and I do not suggest you try "monkey-wrenching," this book provides vicarious thrills and will make you think twice when you come across destruction resulting from mining, logging, ranching, and out-of-control tourism.

Alexander, Taylor R., and George S. Fitcher. *Ecology, A Golden Guide*. Racine, Wisconsin: Western Publishing Company, 1973. Provides a great introduction to the subject. Easy enough for kids to use, too.

Arizona Highways and United States Forest Service. *Mogollon Rim Hiking Map*. 1992. Excellent full-color pamphlet showing several hikes along the Rim. Contains maps, route descriptions, and other information.

Bowman, Eldon, with historical background by Elaine Cassey. *A Guide to the General Crook Trail*. Flagstaff: Museum of Northern Arizona Press and Boy Scouts of America, 1978. This excellent pamphlet describes the entire Crook Trail from Prescott to Fort Apache, with very accurate maps and narrative. If you can find this one, hang on to it!

Chronic, Halka. *Roadside Geology of Arizona*. Missoula, Montana: Mountain Press Publishing Company, 1983. A layperson's description of the geologic processes visible from various roads in the state. Includes Arizona Highway 87 from Pine to Mesa.

Cooley, M. E. *Arizona Highway Geologic Map.* Phoenix: Arizona Geological Society, 1967. This map shows the age of all the surface rocks in Arizona. It also provides an excellent geologic history of the state as well as a listing of important geologic events.

Cornell, Joseph. *Sharing Nature With Children.* Nevada City, California: Dawn Publications, 1979. Great book to help your kids enjoy the outdoors as much as you do. Especially good for doing something after you ride with kids who are still too young to ride themselves.

Dedera, Don. *Arizona's Mogollon Rim.* Phoenix: Arizona Highways, in cooperation with United States Forest Service, 1992. A good overview of the area. Provides a wide range of information, including camping, hiking spots, and a couple of bike rides.

Ellison, Glenn R. "Slim." *Cowboys Under the Rim.* Tucson: University of Arizona Press, 1968. Autobiographical sketches of some interesting events by the son of one of the early pioneers. This book is difficult to find, but is worth locating to help get a feel for what pioneer life was like here.

Fleming, June. *Staying Found: The Complete Map and Compass Handbook.* New York: Vintage Books, 1982. The skills I learned from this easy-to-understand training manual helped me time and again while doing research for this book. No one should go into the wilderness without a map, compass, and a basic understanding of how to use them. If you do not have that skill, buy this book and learn it.

Granger, Byrd Howell. *Arizona's Names (X Marks the Place).* Tucson: Falconer Publishing Company, 1983. Brief histories behind the place-names of a number of locations throughout the state.

Grey, Zane. *Arizona Ames.* New York: Grosset and Dunlap, 1932.
———. *To The Last Man.* Roslyn, New York: Walter J. Black, 1921.
———. *Under the Tonto Rim.* New York: Harper, 1926.
If you haven't read any of Grey's novels, these three are the best to start with. They depict life in the Rim Country before it was tamed and make excellent post-ride reading. Each will make you

want to go out and forge your way through the most remote and difficult trails you can find.

Hanchett, Leland J., Jr. *The Crooked Trail to Holbrook*. Phoenix: Arrowhead Press, Inc., 1993. A well-researched history of the cattle trail from Young to the railroad loading pens in Holbrook, including photographs. Hanchett details the interesting historical events at each of the major stops along the trail.

Lambert, David, and the Diagram Group. *The Field Guide to Geology*. New York: Facts on File, 1988. A brilliant visual introduction to geology. Every page is loaded with detailed drawings and concise descriptions. Anyone, including children, who reads this book and uses it in the field will come away with a comprehensive introduction to geology.

Little, Elbert L. *The Audubon Society Field Guide to North American Trees: Western Region*. New York: Alfred A. Knopf, 1980. Provides comprehensive and detailed descriptions of trees in the western U.S. as well as interesting tidbits of information beyond the strictly biological descriptions.

MacMahon, James A. *Deserts*. New York: Alfred A. Knopf, 1985. This Audubon Society Guide is invaluable for understanding the desert ecosystem of the area. It provides a complete introduction to all of the plants, animals, and insects commonly found here.

Nations, Dale, and Edmund Stump. *Geology of Arizona*. Dubuque, Iowa: Kendall/Hunt Publishing Company, 1981. An academic introduction to geologic processes seen in Arizona. Although difficult to follow, if you know a little about geology this book is a good way to increase your understanding.

Noble, Marguerite. *Filaree*. New York: Random House, 1979. A novel about a young woman and her inept husband in late nineteenth-century Payson.

Northern Gila County Historical Society. *Rim Country History Illustrated*. Payson, Arizona: Rim Country Printery, 1984. A comprehensive history of the Rim Country as told by descendants of original settlers. Although this book is somewhat fragmented and lacks sufficient documentation, it does tell the history of Payson in great detail. Information for many of the historical portions in this guide is culled from this publication.

Robbins, Chandler S., Bertel Bruun, and Herbert S. Zim. *A Guide to Field Identification: Birds of North America*. Racine, Wisconsin: Western Publishing Company, 1966. The most accessible birding book on the market. The maps and song charts are especially helpful for naming any bird you might see or hear in the Rim Country.

Scott, Shirley L. *A Field Guide to the Birds*. 2d ed. Washington, D.C.: National Geographic Society, 1985. The precise color drawings and detailed maps make this beautiful book easy to use. The only drawback is its lack of song charts.

Spellenberg, Richard. *The Audubon Society Field Guide to North American Wildflowers*. New York: Alfred A. Knopf, 1979. Provides comprehensive and detailed descriptions of area wildflowers along with interesting tidbits of information beyond the strictly biological descriptions.

Spicer, Edward H. *Cycles of Conquest: The Impact of Spain, Mexico, and the United States on the Indians of the Southwest, 1533–1960*. Tucson: University of Arizona Press, 1962. A comprehensive study of the acculturation of all major Native American tribes in the Southwest. Although this book touches only marginally and briefly on tribes of the Rim Country, it provides an excellent understanding of the changes brought about in Native American culture as a result of contact with non-natives.

Summerhayes, Martha. *Vanished America: Recollections of the Army Life of a New England Woman*. Salem, Massachusetts: Salem Press, 1911. A vivid personal account of one woman's experience at Fort McDowell, Arizona, and of her rough journey along the General Crook Trail.

United States Department of Agriculture Forest Service. *Apache-Sitgreaves National Forests Map*. 1985.

————. *Tonto National Forest Map.* 1986. Anytime you go into the forest, you should take a forest map along. They show all of the roads where you are allowed to take a motor vehicle as well as major hiking trails. They do not show contour lines, but they provide invaluable help to get you to the start of your ride, or to take you off the beaten track.

Whitaker, John O., Jr. *The Audubon Society Field Guide to North American Mammals.* New York: Alfred A. Knopf, 1980. Provides comprehensive and detailed descriptions of mammals you might see in the Rim Country. The book also provides interesting tidbits of information beyond the strictly biological descriptions.

Whitney, Stephan. *Western Forests.* New York: Alfred A. Knopf, 1985. This Audubon Society Guide is invaluable for understanding forest ecosystems of the area. It provides a complete introduction to all of the plants, animals, and insects commonly found here.

Anecdotal information was gathered from a variety of sources. In particular, I would like to recognize the following libraries for their help and suggest that you visit them to learn more about the Rim Country:

The Arizona Historical Foundation, Arizona State University, Tempe, Arizona 85287.

The Arizona Mining and Mineral Museum, 1502 West Washington, Phoenix, Arizona 85007.

The Hayden Library, Department of Archives and Manuscripts, Tempe, Arizona.

Index